TEILHARD DE CHARDIN: RE-MYTHOLOGIZATION

Three papers on the thought of
Teilhard de Chardin
presented at a symposium at
Seabury-Western Theological Seminary
Evanston, Illinois
September, 1968
By
Robert Speaight
Robert V. Wilshire
J. V. Langmead Casserly

WORD BOOKS, Publisher
Waco, Texas

ACKNOWLEDGMENTS

Grateful acknowledgment is made to Harper and Row Publishers, Inc., for permission to reprint excerpts from *The Phenomenon of Life* by Hans Jonas, Copyright 1966, and to the University of Chicago Press and Robert Kimball, literary executor of the Tillich estate, for permission to reprint excerpts from *Systematic Theology* by Paul Tillich, Volumes I, II, III, Copyright 1951, 1957, 1963, University of Chicago Press.

Library of Congress Catalog Card Number: 73-113275

Contents

Introduction

1. Teilhard de Chardin the Man
   by Robert Speaight

2. Teilhard de Chardin as Theologian
   by J. V. Langmead Casserly

3. Teilhard de Chardin as Philosopher
   by Robert V. Wilshire

design by Patricia Ellen Ricci

Illustrations for Casserly section are negative prints of Dore Illustrations of Dante's Divine Comedy

Introduction

TO LOVE THE WORLD: Implications for Remythologization
In The Thought of Teilhard de Chardin

THE THREE ESSAYS which constitute this book are the partial
result of an ecumenical conference held at Seabury-Western
Theological Seminary, Evanston, Illinois, in September 1968
which was concerned with the broad theme, "Teilhard de Chardin
and the Future of Man." As the conference progressed the papers
and discussion made it abundantly clear that the "future of man"
was inextricably bound to the quest for meaning, the prevailing
struggle in the life of modern man. Meaning, however, is the function of myth and as such it poses for modern man in general and
the modern Christian in particular the crucial dilemma: Is he to
find a "new" myth or can he locate within his culture adequate

5

means whereby he can express anew the myth which has served as his guide for nearly twenty centuries?

The crisis of myth obviously points to the estrangement between God and His creation, the burden of which is increasingly felt by modern man. This predicament stands as a testimonial of sorts to theology's preoccupation with "God who addresses man" to the exclusion of the one addressed. The solution is not to be found in more talk *about* God. The problem is not one of how to talk *about* God; rather, it is more intimate, more urgent: How may man address God?

The task of theology in our present age is to take account not only of God but of His creation as well. This does not necessitate a turning away from God to an anthropology *per se.* Such a procedure would constitute for the Christian a new myth, or more correctly, a fable. It is not a matter of *either/or,* but of *both/and.* Viewed from this perspective, it is possible to visualize how man might live and find meaning within the present myth by making it more inclusive — inclusive of creation and man, himself.

Whether such a proposal will be accepted by theology is another matter. The distrust of the world and of man runs deep not only within the Christian tradition but within the general culture as well. No matter how many times one recalls "God so loved the world", the idea that one can really love the world and rejoice in it is still very much a matter of grave doubt to many. Yet it remains a possibility, and, as such, it offers hope to the problem of finding meaning in our lives. That is, after all, the promise of the Gospel.

One man who saw the possibility of rejoicing in the world and acted upon it was Pierre Teilhard de Chardin, the French Jesuit paleontologist. His life — his thoughts and feelings — have been cogently highlighted in Robert Speaight's biographical sketch, "Teilhard the Man", the first essay in this present work. As the British biographer and critic points out, Teilhard was a man intensely interested in the creation and in everything human. Behind all of his work as well as the direction of his life one senses an unspoken motto: "To Love the World."

His concern for the world enabled Teilhard to reflect theologically with a vigor that often led critics to scorn his theology and to scoff at his science. And yet it was this attitude which, nevertheless, reopened a "closed myth" in order that the world might be included. In so doing, Teilhard found "in the prevailing secular culture a set of words and ideas in which the gospel drama of faith and salvation can be vividly set forth . . ." And as Dr. J. V. Langmead Casserley, theology professor at Seabury-Western, reminds us in the second essay, "Teilhard de Chardin As Theologian", this is the supreme theological problem — *remythologization.*

Remythologization is not a part of the Teilhardian vocabulary, but it does provide a perspective for evaluating the man and his thought. The Reverend Robert W. Wilshire in the concluding essay, "Teilhard de Chardin as Philosopher of History", pursues further the implications of remythologizing content in Teilhard's attempt to find a nexis between God and the world. Dr. Wilshire is professor at General Theological Seminary, New York.

To "love the world" is not to create a new myth. It is but a stance toward God which is significantly aware of the implications of God's love for the world. To love God is to love the world, and herein is the possibility for meaning and for hope of a future for mankind.

Seabury-Western Seminary   Thomas Oman Edmunds
Evanston, Illinois

In terms of 'energy' and biology, the human race is still very young and very fresh.

Teilhard de Chardin –
The Man

By ROBERT SPEAIGHT

IT IS A PRIVILEGE and a pleasure to introduce these thoughts on
Pierre Teilhard de Chardin, but my qualifications for doing
so are modest. I am not a philosopher, a theologian, or a paleontologist. I am not even a Jesuit. I am merely a biographer who has
tried to set the thought of Teilhard in the context of his character
and his life.

With some thinkers this might not seem so important. With
Teilhard we are likely to go astray if we separate the thinker from
the man; what is valuable or defective in his thought derives
from his temperament and from his career.

Teilhard said he was not an expert philosopher or theologian,
and many philosophers and theologians agree with him in this,
if in nothing else. He was a paleontologist, of this there was never

any question. Yet if he had been no more than a paleontologist, we would not be gathered here in his name.

We listen to him not because he constructed a water-tight system, as did Aquinas or Marx, but because his reasoning and his intuitions, however difficult to understand or to accept, however partial or provisional, however imperfectly formulated, have the life-blood of experience behind them. He sees — and how profoundly he sees — because he has learned to observe; and the observer is inseparable from the observation.

My first introduction to Teilhard was through the *Milieu Divin,* in a copy passed to me, so to speak, under the counter. I do not understand the necessity for this subterfuge. The next time I heard of Teilhard was when I was in Paris in the summer of 1945. I was lunching with Madame Roland de Margerie who had known him well in Peking. She showed me a fragment of *La Messe sur le Monde,* and I was so impressed by this that I begged her to copy it for me. I had a number of copies printed, rather beautifully. One copy now hangs in the sacristy of Campion Hall at Oxford. I sent a copy to Teilhard himself.

When Teilhard returned to Paris in the summer of 1946 he invited me to the Rue Monsieur where he was staying. I knocked on the door of his room. The door opened and he came out with his arms outstretched, exclaiming: "Monsieur, I am confused." He could not understand why I had come to have his text so elaborately inscribed. I saw the gift 20 years later hanging on the walls of his devoted secretary, Mlle. Jeanne Mortier. He had bequeathed it to her.

THE UPWARD SLOPE OF FAME

Teilhard was 65 years old when I met him. His health and vigor were unimpaired, but he felt himself "on the downward slope of life." Nevertheless, he was on the upward slope of fame. His return to Paris had been greeted with headlines in the newspapers; he was besieged by visitors. A younger generation hung upon his words.

As we talked in the garden after luncheon, heads hung out of windows to catch what Teilhard was saying. Yet at this time, you could not go into a book-store and buy a copy of Teilhard's works. His message had been diffused by word of mouth and by the circulation of his "under-the-counter" manuscripts. He later described those first three months after his return to Paris as the happiest of his life. It was the right moment to have caught him.

Teilhard was a Parisian even before he was a Frenchman, and it had been eight years since he had been in Paris. It had been 20 years since he had had the right to work there. Paris was the arena of the world's debate. Marxists met him on the one hand and the existentialists on the other; and he was never happier than in the company of people with whom he disagreed. He rarely disagreed with them entirely, for he had a genius for finding the patch of common ground, without yielding an inch of disputed territory.

In this sense he was a genuine collectivist, because he believed that men must advance together, in a mutual adventure of research, sharing their discoveries and learning from their mistakes; and in so far as they went forward they would converge. With the Marxists he had been on excellent terms. "And when your state has withered away, and your millennium of human happiness has been secured," he would argue, "what then?"

Because the Marxists had no answer to the riddle of death and spiritual destiny, Teilhard found their philosophy insufficient — ardently as he shared their faith in the future and in the pursuit of happiness, if happiness were rightly understood. In Peking, he had found conversation with the Communist guerillas on the other side of the hills more entertaining than the chit-chat of diplomatic cocktail parties.

11

It has become fashionable today to mock on to treat with suspicion, anything which looks like faith in the future. If we are not careful this skepticism will be fatal, for its direct result is to destroy both the love of living and the momentum of mankind.

The existentialist was a new and less congenial opponent. Teilhard, cut off from the agonies of Europe and even from those who could have told him about them, found it difficult to believe in the tragic absurdity of life.

There were moments, nevertheless, when he was tempted to despair. As the manuscript of *The Phenomenon of Man* languished on the desks of uncomprehending superiors, he wondered if his message would ever get through. It is important to remember that Teilhard was an apostle and an apologist, anxious above all to persuade and to communicate, and it was his life-long ordeal that communication, in the sense that he wished, was forbidden him. Often, we are told, in those long years of exile, he was brought to tears. Yet, for him, hope was supreme. What he said would only matter when others had bettered his instruction.

Our conversation, that afternoon in the garden of the Rue Monsieur, turned to the atom bomb. Here, surely, was occasion for despair. Teilhard could hardly have foreseen so rapid or catastrophic a conquest of atomic energy; yet the catastrophe was only incidental to the conquest. And so, even in the face of these appalling possibilities, he would hear nothing of despair.

TEILHARD THE MYSTIC

There can be no doubt that in some sense or other Teilhard was a mystic, if by mystic we mean one who has had direct experience of Absolute Reality. How far, in his case, was the experience of the natural or supernatural kind? I doubt whether a definite answer will ever be given.

We know that Teilhard's cosmic Christology owed everything to St. John and St. Paul; we know that he was at opposite poles from Modernism in his postulate of a transcendent God. We know, too, that he was aware of a temptation to pantheism, which he overcame as his thought matured and theology — how-

His own attitude, not only to politics but to much else besides, has been described as "passionate indifference." The phrase must be carefully understood; it does not mean that he was insensitive, only that he was detached. This detachment was the fruit of a dual discipline: the discipline of the Order to which he remained faithful even unto death, and the discipline which the frustrations of his career had imposed upon him. Moreover, he viewed events in the light of the future — a distant and hardly imaginable future — upon which his vision was suspended.

It was not that Teilhard was disinterested in what was happening today, but he was more interested in what would happen tomorrow. You could not meet him for five minutes without realizing how human he was, but he was not in the least humanitarian. Neither war, nor pestilence, nor personal anxiety were meaningless tragedies; they could all be turned to advantage in "building the earth."

He had known much of war, and he had won every possible decoration for valor in World War I. He had stumbled deep in the mud of Flanders and had come unscathed through the carnage of Verdun. He had braved the perils of No Man's Land to bring back the body of a comrade. He had heard the confessions of men who might be killed a few minutes later, as he might be killed himself.

Pierre Rousselot, perhaps the greatest theologian of his generation, who shared and partly inspired Teilhard's belief in the consistence of the Universe in Christ, had given his life in the same catastrophe.

But for Teilhard there was no such thing as a senseless catastrophe. In spite of his compassion for individual suffering — and to this there were no limits — he saw the agonies and edurances of the present as the matrix of the future, and the future would justify them. Writing, as he wrote all his early essays, in reserve billets, he spoke of his "nostalgia for the front," and some were

15

Our modern world was created in less than ten thousand years, and in the last two hundred years it has changed faster than in all the previous milleniums.

shocked. Notice that he did not write "nostalgia for the war." For him, the front was more than blood-stained ribbons of trenches and barbed wire. It was the extreme limit and most incandescent point of human effort, and for this reason it was a place Teilhard wanted to be.

WAR: A PLUNGE INTO REALITY

"The war," he told a friend, "finally took me out of my books, and away from my colleagues, from a superior moral and intellectual milieu . . . and plunged me into the tragic realities of mud and blood, into a magma of every race and class and kind. In doing this it gave me the baptism of reality which I so badly needed and from which I learned so much. This explains the nostalgia for the front, about which I wrote and spoke, and that I felt whenever I relapsed into the humdrum routine of everyday life. You mustn't be scandalized. Above all, you mustn't think that I wasn't shattered by the sufferings and the death of my comrades in the trenches. But for all the aching of my heart, I felt what I have never felt since and what I have missed, the great purifying breath of courage, of union, of "communion," which passed over us in contact with death. In the trenches we were no longer isolated individuals, each with his personal life. We were riveted to one another in a single, immense *Unity,* in a collective body, whose perils, and physical and moral sufferings we shared in equal brotherhood. This is what I found exalting."

Teilhard had been a very long way from the front in Peking, but now in Paris he felt a good deal nearer. The war of armies was over, but the war of ideas was raging. Teilhard was happy to be in the midst of this.

Not all the existentialists were atheists. I remember a conversation with Gabriel Marcel shortly after Teilhard's return to Paris. Teilhard had given a lecture on *"L'Homme Communautaire",* and for Marcel this had totalitarian overtones. "I confess," he said to me, "that Teilhard sends me back to St. Thomas," and Marcel's philosophy, which he had refused to synthesize, was at the antipodes of Thomism.

Teilhard and Marcel entered into friendly dialogue, Marcel refusing to see a necessary spiritual advance in technological progress and quoting the doctors at Dachau for his purpose, and Teilhard arguing — not very carefully — that man to be truly man had to try everything. To Marcel and many others the genocide of the Jews seemed rather more than a necessary flaw in the evolutionary process.

Perhaps the thinker to whom Teilhard was closest was Emmanuel Mounier. Mounier's distinction between the person and the individual met Teilhard's thought at many points. It offered a *via media* which sanctioned the socialization of mankind without turning mankind into an ant-heap. Moreover, Mounier was interested in practical politics, and also in psychology, in a way that Teilhard was not. A man of leonine courage and heroic faith, he had been through all those years of controversy and conflict, deeply committed.

VALUE IN COMPETING IDEOLOGIES

In the First World War Teilhard's "passionate indifference" was a triumph of mind over emotion; in the second, distance gave him an easier detachment. He could see something of value in all the competing ideologies. He admired the faith of the Communists, however limited, and the energy of the Fascists, however misdirected. Against these the undecided democracies were like antiquated dreadnaughts. He detested nationalism in any form, and he disliked the Iron Curtain, already in process of construction, because it shut the Russians in upon themselves.

He was no believer in racial equality, which is not to say that he countenanced racial discrimination. He thought it danger-

18

ous to deny biological evidence in the name of liberal idealism. When he was in Ethiopia he described the natives as "magnificent bronze animals," and he maintained the right of more developed nations to assist, forcibly if need be, the progress of more primitive peoples. The kingdoms of the earth, as well as the Kingdom of Heaven, had occasionally to be taken by storm.

This brings me to another reason for Teilhard's happiness when I met him that day in Paris. He was a Westerner to the marrow of his bones. Some Europeans find their spiritual home elsewhere — in India, maybe, or in China. But Teilhard's long sojourn in the East was a spiritual as well as a geographical exile. Even with his Chinese collaborators in the laboratory at Peking he was never completely at ease. He was irked by their agnostic pragmatism, their impenetrable reserve. With the passive spirituality of the East he had no sympathy, and the Chinese masses he regarded, quite simply, as inferior stuff.

He was generally impervious to Chinese art. The porcelain was merely decorative. As for the wooden temples and pagodas, cathedrals should be made of stone, and houses too. He had no taste for the flimsy or the fragile or the fleeting; the works of man should imitate the permanence of the works of God. It was the same in India where the distinctions of caste seemed to him a repellent and retrograde superstition, and the erotic sculpture a degraded symbol of cosmic energy.

If there is a single word that gives us a clue to Teilhard's character it is energy. The boy collecting his "stones" from the river beds of Auvergne; the scholastic in search of fossils in the Egyptian desert or digging up a tooth of "Piltdown Man" in the Sussex Weald; the geologist of the Gobi and the explorer of the Croisiere Jaune. Always he seemed to be in movement, trekking through the Burmese jungle and refusing the comforts to which age and prestige entitled him. Follow him from year to year, and you see him on the uplands of Ethiopia, or drifting in a boat down

19

The universe is ripening within itself the fruit of a certain consciousness.

the Red Sea, or hunting for the origins of man in what used to be known as darkest Africa. The brief moments of repose were merely springboards for the next adventure.

DIALOG BETWEEN THOUGHT AND ACTION

His whole life was a dialogue between thought and action, the one feeding on the other, and neither at rest for very long. Not for him the Sphinx-like Buddhas and enervating passivities of the Orient; even the Cross was a symbol of energy rather than resignation. "We should climb with its struggle," he wrote, "and not swoon in its shadow." No man more amply fulfilled his family motto: "Fiery their force and heavenly their home."

And yet we should not forget — as Teilhard never forgot — that he had a home on earth as well. Sarcenat was a home even if, as we read the record of his endless itinerary, it seems little more than a cradle. In fact, he carried it with him wherever he went. If he walked in the Bois de Boulogne he wished it were the brushwood of Auvergne. The basaltic plateau of Jehol and the woods and pastures of Weighang reminded him of the Puys-de-Dome, except that irises instead of gentians grew under his feet.

It was at his brother's house in Auvergne that Teilhard recuperated after his heart attack in 1948, and on his last visit to France in 1953 he made a pilgrimage to Sarcenat. His mother and father were dead; one of his sisters had died of the small-pox in Shanghai, and the other had died after a long illness heroically borne; of his four brothers only one was still alive. The family which had once gathered for prayers in the old chateau among its chestnuts, limes, and young elms, and hunted the snipe in the marshes of the Allier, had been decimated. Teilhard was not the man to indulge his emotions, but when he got to Sarcenat, where his widowed sister-in-law and her family were the sole occupants, he stayed for only a quarter of an hour.

21

His invalid sister Marguerite-Marie had called her book *The Spiritual Energy of Suffering*. She could not have chosen a more Teilhardian title. Yet their destinies had been dramatically different — she immobilized, he in continual movement — and God alone knew, he wrote in the Preface to that book, which had had the better part.

Teilhard illustrated both the family's patrician style and its military virtues. Immensely tall; the face refined and chiselled; his expression intent, and veiled, now and then, with detachment or irony, lit up with humor, affection, or curiosity; the body lithe, alert, and stretching forward. This inclination of the body was something quite different from the scholar's stoop. Teilhard's manner was simple, self-deprecating, and unpretentious. "Of course, I may be wrong" he would say in concluding an argument, and then add with a twinkle "but I don't think so."

He was perfectly at ease in any company; a man of the world, because the world was his business, and because God had created it and found it "very good." He knew how to listen as well as to talk, — a faculty rather rare in people with strong opinions; and indeed you might say of his message that it was an answer to other people's questions as well as to his own.

He was fortunate in his friends, and Teilhard had a genius for friendship. There was Auguste Valensin, the disciple of Maurice Blondel and a great Dante scholar. They had been through the novitiate together, and although their paths rarely crossed in later years, Valensin was always ready with advice in time of trouble. Teilhard wrote nothing without inviting his correction. Valensin was among the greatest of the many great men the Society of Jesus has given to the twentieth century. I met him the same year that I met Teilhard, and I regret that we never met again, for my own interests lie rather closer to Valensin than to Teilhard. Some people are born Teilhardian; some achieve Teilhardism; and some have Teilhard thrust upon them. In a very real sense I had Teilhard thrust upon me when I was asked to write his biography. For my natural disposition is to regard the past with tenderness, the present with distaste, and the future with dismay. These are scarcely Teilhardian attitudes.

To the End — With a Smile

If, as I believe, strong personalities are formed by the tension between the individual and the institution, Teilhard is an example very much to the point. When he was silenced by his Roman — not his French — superiors in 1926, because they thought him unorthodox on the question of Original Sin, many people, both then and afterwards, urged him to leave the Society. If he stayed he would have to combine external conformity with interior dissent. Might not those who had looked to him for advice, and whose doubts over a difficult doctrine he had done his best to resolve, accuse him of intellectual cowardice? Was it worth stifling the diffusion of his message for the sake of *esprit de corps?* After all, his old schoolmaster, Henri Bremond, had left the Society and written his classic history of religious thought in France during the seventeenth century.

Teilhard had taken his final vows, but from these he could obtain dispensation. As the years went by, he was refused permission to publish *The Divine Milieu* and *The Phenomenon of Man,* in spite of untiring efforts to meet the objections of the censors; refused permission to accept a chair at the College de France; chased not only from Paris but even from Shanghai because he was thought to be intellectually contagious — as, Heaven knows, he was; denied the right to have such articles as had appeared with ecclesiastical permission translated into German. As he reflected on all this and saw the prospect of communicating his ideas receding day by day, he must have wondered whether his patience and his perseverance had been worth while. Why, therefore, did he decide to "go on to the end, and with a smile if possible?"

I thank you my God. for having in a thousand different ways led my eyes to discover the immense simplicity of things.

The answer was given by Teilhard: "When I took my vows I committed myself. To break them would be an offense against honor."

"One must work from within," he said. "Those who leave," Teilhard went on "no longer have any influence."

"The spirit of the Church is changing little by little," he said. "For me, this is something quite certain. The day when a scientist sits beside the theologians in Rome, the ideas now considered revolutionary will be generally accepted. . . . The day will come; there can be no possible doubt about it. If St. Thomas were living today he would be the first to rewrite his *Summa*. And who knows whether, as a result of some discovery, my own books will have to be rewritten later?"

UNDAUNTED FAITH IN HUMAN PROGRESS

Teilhard had his eyes so fixed on the future that he could afford to wait. In the world of thought, progress was infinitely slow, but already the evolutionism of Darwin and Lamarck looked crudely linear and it would be childish to return to it. Already theology was adapting itself to the world of ascertained phenomena, and representing Divinity, without any concessions to a minimizing modernism, in a way that the world could understand. The Christus Pantacrator of Byzantium was none the less transcendent because he was also Christ the Worker "building the earth," very often alongside those who did not believe in him. It was a mistake to believe that the masses would be won by beneficence; they would be won by hope, and this was what Christianity could bring them.

"The Christian," said Teilhard, "can believe in progress far more thoroughly than the Marxist, for he knows that at the end of life there is not a wall and a nothingness. There is an escape, a change of condition, an ascent towards a summit." This was the hope, this was the ineffable expectation, which sustained Teilhard

25

through his long ordeal of submission. "I am faithful to everything I have been taught," he said, "although I realize that those who taught me did not perhaps know the full significance of their teaching. Fidelity and obedience have been, and still are, the major imperatives of my religious life."

If the Jesuits of the Roman Curia were slow in acknowledging their debt to Teilhard, he was not unaware of his debt to the Society and in particular to its founder. His great friend and fellow-scientist, Abbe Breuil, wrote of what he called "the miracle of the Jesuits." This consisted in a complete submission to authority and at the same time a complete liberty of soul. Teilhard was able to maintain his obedience and also to preserve intact the fidelity to his own thought and his right as a priest to make it known. The protection of his Order was the price he had to pay for a silence to be broken only by his death, and it would have been unavailing if he had not been an exemplary religious, speaking his mind fearlessly and yet doing as he was told. A secular priest, undefended by a powerful society and enjoying the freedom of publication, would have very quickly seen his books on the Index if he had written as Teilhard wrote in the theological climate of his time.

Teilhard's position was singular in as much as he was more than usually exposed to secular contacts. There was Marcellin Boule, an invincible sceptic. Teilhard was descended on one side of his family from Pascal and on the other from Voltaire, so he had a healthy respect for scepticism. There was Davidson Black, the Canadian, who presided over the discovery of Sinanthropus and died at his desk in the Peking laboratory, and whom Teilhard mourned as a brother. There was George Barbour, a Presbyterian Scot, with whom he explored the upper reaches of the Yangtse, and who has left us so vivid a description of Teilhard in the field.

TEILHARD IN THE FIELD: A PORTRAIT

"He exchanged his clerical garb for a khaki drill suit of military cut with four tunic pockets. A folding penknife, hand lens, marching compass, and loose money went into his trouser pockets. The padlock key of his kit-box was on a loop of string in his watch pocket. Bank-notes and his passport went in an inside breast pocket, because the left upper pocket always carried his breviary, while the right one held matches and a crushed packet of Job or Gauloise cigarettes. The right side pocket held his small shiny black note-book with graph paper. The contents of the left pocket varied with the occasion: a folded map, a piece of string, a chip of lava, a fossil wrapped in newspaper, or even an unfinished square of chocolate wrapped in silver paper . . . .

"When we arrived for the night and had found a spot for our folding camp cots, the cook would start a fire, and then forage for noodles, eggs, an occasional chicken, and turnips which tasted like pears. Our wooden supply box — which came home loaded with rocks and fossils — furnished the extras: sugar, coffee, condensed milk, confiture, marmalade, tinned fruit, chocolate, candles, matches, and insect lotion. By the time we had washed up and changed shirts, water was boiling for a cup of tea. Teilhard would then hunt for his brown felt pantoufles with the red stripes, light a cigarette and relax. . . . After supper he would light another cigarette and I would take out my pipe. Then, while he was completing his field notes for the day, we would compare conclusions while they were fresh in our minds and lay plans for the morrow."

As night fell and the camp fire burned low, the French Jesuit would talk to the Scots Presbyterian of the ideas which he was putting down in his essays and letters. The challenge of Marxist materialism, the inertia of the Church, the poverty and almost sub-human ignorance of the peasants among whom they had made their bivouac — the conversation was at once a meditation — as St. Ignatius had written in a text which Teilhard never

OUR DUTY AS MEN IS TO PROCEED
AS IF LIMITS TO OUR ABILITY DID
NOT EXIST. WE ARE COLLABORATORS
IN CREATION.

ever liberally interpreted — imposed its distinctions. But that first intuition of the Absolute which came to him as a boy when he played truant "to discover what was inside the volcanoes," and saluted "the god of iron" which disappointed him because it was liable to rust — that insistent search for the Sacred Heart of Jesus — this had something in common with Wordsworth, but went, I think, far beyond Wordsworth.

Among mystical writers Saint Teresa was his life-long preference. He thought, in opposition to Maurice Blondel, that the drastic counsels of St. John of the Cross would turn the world into a monastery, and Teilhard was the least monastic of men. Just as the cosmic Christ of evolution, clothing the point Omega of its term with Divine Personality, tended to diminish, although in no way to deny, the Jesus of history, so the Christ to whom St. Teresa could observe "I am not surprised that you have so few friends considering the way you treat them" was the object of Teilhard's devotion, rather than the Ineffable Deity to be grasped through a cloud of unknowing.

Teilhard coined a number of abstract nouns, many of them awkward and some of them hardly intelligible, but his mysticism, like his mind, was anchored in the concrete. If we ask ourselves whether his mysticism was of the natural or the supernatural kind, that is because he clung to these categories less rigidly than his critics. "Supernatural" — not to be equated with "spiritual" — was a word which he thought might well be given a rest.

BUILDING THE EARTH — WITH DETACHMENT

At the time when I met him, Sartre and Camus were the spokesmen of a fashionable existentialism. Both had proved their courage in the French Resistance of World War II, while Teilhard was too far above the *melee* to know what it was about. He was to that extent uncommitted during a decade of passionate commitment.

14

ceased to ponder, a *meditatio ad amorem* — and a mutual inquiry; and it continued until the smoke of Teilhard's last Gauloise had evaporated into the thin air.

As his thought deepened and his very competent English failed to respond to it, Teilhard would slide into his native tongue, but even Teilhard's French was not always adequate to the complexity of his ideas. Mgr. de Nedoncelle has said that "he had a natural and disarming indifference for the verbal police, tailoring afresh for his own use the language of other people. He never put on the frock coat of his ancestors; he piously left it in the cupboard." And so fatigue would at last overtake him, and unless his breviary detained him he would turn in for the night.

Another witness described him as "a man of unequalled style; of a self-effacing and irresistible distinction. His voice, his diction which had the tone of a harpsichord, his smile which never quite turned to laughter, impressed themselves on anyone who was in the least attentive. A total lack of ecclesiasticism. He was simple in his gestures as in his manners. . . . Anxious to welcome, but like a rock of marble. You felt that even if you were as tall as he, you were still infinitely far removed from the storehouse of his thoughts which were never inflated. As a rule you stopped dead before that rough-hewn face that Greco had prefigured, and you fell back on the ordinary chit-chat of the expedition."

These men did not share Teilhard's religious beliefs, Now and again the conversation turned on the existence of God. "God" said Teilhard "is like a note of music" — and his hand traced a spiral in the air.

> "The man that hath no music in his soul
> And is not moved by concord of sweet sounds
> Is fit for treasons, strategems and spoils;
> Let no such man be trusted."

It was not a bad way of communicating one's beliefs to an agnostic.

One day in Peking Teilhard complained to his friend Pierre Leroy: "I have too many petticoats around me." In plain English, women ran after Teilhard de Chardin; he did not necessarily run away from them. Protected by the vow of chastity, he claimed the rights of creative friendship. There was his cousin Marguerite Teilhard-Chambon who had been given to him, he said, "for the war" and whose friendship he also compared to "a note of music." There were others in whom he could not help arousing expectations which he was unable to fulfill. One of these, at least, caused him a period of serious strain. Everything in Teilhard was virile, just as everything was pure, and "l'Eternal Feminin" — as he described her in an early essay — had to be accommodated in his life as well as in his thought. He had to justify as well as to practice virginity. You will find his doctrine set out in the essay I have just mentioned, and in a later essay, as yet unpublished, *L'Evolution de la Chastete.*

L'Eternel Feminin is rather mysteriously dedicated to "Beatrix," and the connection with Beatrice in Dante's *Divine Comedy* is clear. For Beatrice was the mediatrix between human and divine love. She is the "charm" introduced into the world to assist its grouping, as well as "the ideal suspended above it" to encourage its ascent.

The Evolution of Chastity was composed when Teilhard's thought had stood the test of personal experience. He certainly had a higher opinion of women than St. Paul — which is not saying much; he maintained that on the intellectual plane feminine intuition and sensibility were an indispensable complement to the rational judgment of men. And there was a spiritual power in the flesh itself, a "withinness," which was "the heart of the matter."

Chastity, in the Christian tradition, had been tainted with a contempt for matter, and for a long time the union of the sexes had been approved for reproductive purposes alone. Teilhard of course, would have none of this. He only touched obliquely on the problem of birth control, but he pleaded for a healthy eugenics. The command to increase and multiply had once made scientific sense; it made sense no longer. When the *Osservatore Romano* talked about "colonies of virgins" and "currents of continence in marriage" Teilhard thought that one could not "play more frankly with the limits of psychological forces, nor rely more absolutely on the power of a faith that one was doing everything possible to make anaemic." These words have a certain relevance today.

Teilhard naturally admitted the corruptive influence of sexuality; of all the forces of matter woman was the most to be feared. But danger was in itself a symptom of power. There was no reason to dispense with fire because fire consumed, or with electricity because it was liable to create explosions. If he had to choose between avoiding a mistake at the risk of impoverishment or seeking enrichment at the risk of a scratch or two, he did not hesitate to prefer the second.

For all this, however, he did not question the value of virginity, if virginity were properly understood; for something was lost as well as gained in the ecstasy of physical desire. Here, as always for Teilhard, what mattered was union. "It is in union" he wrote "that man and woman should ascend to God. Spirituality rests upon the human *dyade,* not upon the human *monade."* So it was with this in mind that he sought the partners of his quest, often out-stripping them, knowing himself a master of his own tensions, but aware of his responsibility to other people. "The only possible friend," he discovered was, "one who finds elsewhere, deep within herself, a serious stability in a full life, or in some great ideal."

A GREAT AND COMPLETE MAN

So there you have him — "a great and complete man," as Shakespeare's Ulysses said of Achilles. For Pierre Teilhard de

May the risen Christ keep us young.
That is optimistic, active, smiling,
perceptive.

Chardin the whole of life was a battlefield, and the phenomenon of man was a continuing struggle towards closer union, wider knowledge, and deeper consciousness.

Some may have thought him indifferent to the casualties, but let us not forget that he bore his share of scars.

Did he under-rate the wastage of evolution, the false starts and the dead-ends? Did he too readily equate them with the necessities of growth, the reduction of the multiple to the one, as creation itself, he believed, was in some sense the reduction of multiplicity? Was he too slow to recognize, and too optimistic to explain, the incurable perversity of human nature? Following Newman in so much else, did he shrink from following him back to the "vast aboriginal calamity?" These are questions to which you will no doubt try to bring an answer.

Again, you may think that his historical sense was weak, and that he was so obsessed with the forward movement of mankind that he made too little allowance for disaster and decline. Should not the notion of progress be taken out of time, so that we can think of Shakespeare and Socrates and Mozart as ahead of us — miles and perhaps millenia ahead of us — rather than behind? In terms of our approach to Omega is not time an irrelevance and an illusion? At certain moments Teilhard seems to have realized this; at others he would tie us to "tomorrow and tomorrow and tomorrow" and the "petty pace that creeps in from day to day" — not that the "petty pace" had anything in common with his own gigantic and visionary stride.

I have spoken of his indifference to Chinese art and architecture, and in truth he was indifferent to art in general. This wsa surprising in one who was himself a considerable artist when he was not entangled in his neologisms, and whose response to natural beauty was so quick. But he did not understand why art and poetry and music were so important to so many people; he did not see their analogy with the creative act or, as he would have preferred to call it, the creative process. He stifled among the monuments of the past when their link with the present had been severed.

Teilhard preferred the skyscrapers of Shanghai to the pagodas of Peking, and the throbbing of the cyclotron at Berkeley was sweeter music to his ear than the anguish of Beethoven's quartets. Here was not the "still sad music of humanity," as the poets and musicians had composed it for us, but the hopes and potential of humanity in the way of hitherto unimaginable fulfillment. "Mathematical speculation, laboratory research, the wide scope of industrial enterprises, military ambition, medical hopes of therapy — and even the secret hope of finding the ultimate explanation of things." As the monstrous engine distilled its monstrous energy, the man who had so often spoken about "the mysticism of research" saw "the whole noosphere which, coiled in upon itself by the breath of research, formed a single and enormous cyclone, whose property it was to produce not nuclear energy, but psychic energy in a continually more reflective state, in other words the ultra-human itself. And what was remarkable was that, faced by this colossal reality that should have made my mind reel, I experienced on the contrary a calm and joy — a *deep-seated* calm and joy."

Bent But Not Broken

It is tempting to leave him there, like Moses on the mountain or Elias in his chariot, a secular prophet on the summit of a California hill. No doubt that is the way his secular admirers will wish to see him. But the picture would be incomplete. It would leave out of account the man bent with age, but unbroken in mind and unembittered by disappointment, making his last retreat and asking to be kept young for the greater glory of God, because trials and age came from him and led to him; praying now with

34

his face to the wall, because the future held nothing to which he could look forward, except a death in Christ.

He had prayed to be allowed to die on the day of Resurrection, for which Good Friday was only the prelude. On Easter Sunday 1955 he was apparently in good health and the best of spirits. He said Mass as usual, attended High Mass in St. Patrick's Cathedral, and walked in Central Park. He went to a concert in the afternoon and then had tea with a friend. It was there, standing upright with the cup in his hand, that he fell unconscious to the ground, like a soldier struck by a bullet.

When they came to bury him at St. Andrews on the Hudson, besides his brothers in the Society of Jesus, the "matter" which he had so adored for its consistency was too hard to receive his body, and the body lay in a vault until the ground grew softer. Only a handful of people were present at his Requiem, and only his friend Pierre Leroy and a priest from St. Ignatius' Church escorted the casket to the cemetery. But it was not long before the audience had begun to gather. It is gathering still and we are proud to be a part of it.

Teilhard de Chardin
As Theologian

By J. V. LANGMEAD CASSERLY

"Yet as a wheel moves smoothly, free from jars,
My will and my desire were turned by love,
The love that moves the sun and the other stars."

*   *   *   *   *

THESE CLOSING LINES of *The Divine Comedy,* from the "Sayers
Reynolds" translation of *The Paradiso* are perhaps peculiarly
appropriate to the life and work of Teilhard de Chardin.

As so often with genius it is difficult to place him in his
appropriate category. Was he a scientist? He certainly worked long
and hard in an important department of science, was a man of
broad scientific education and acquitted himself scientifically with
considerable distinction.

It all depends how we define the term. If the word scientist indicates where a man starts rather than where he ends up, Teilhard certainly was a scientist. If the word scientist connotes, as for Sir Peter Medawar in his now famous criticism of Teilhard, something narrow cramping and rigid which surrounds and hems in the mind, Teilhard was not a scientist.

Was he a mystic? If we mean by the word mystic one who stands in the midst of God's world with a mind wide open to every evidence of His glory, Teilhard was not only a mystic but a very great mystic indeed, the author of at least one book, *"The Divine Milieu"* which is to the twentieth century what the works of St. Theresa or St. John of the Cross were to the seventeenth century. But if by the word mystic we mean a man remote and withdrawn, for whom nothing except the religious has any significance at all, then Teilhard was not a mystic.

Was he a theologian? The conventional notion of a theologian that has established itself in Luther's Germany, and wherever else German theology is influential reduces all theology to erudite biblical study and interpretation, a strange blend of scholarly exegesis and speculative hermeneutics. From this point of view Teilhard was not a theologian, and he is even taken to task by Bentz for neglecting to read any German theology at all.

He was almost certainly guilty as charged. And yet in a strange way Teilhard had a sort of intuitive sympathy with the Bible which we do not find in many erudite exegetes. The kind of biblical study for which all questions concerning Christian belief are to be settled by a scholarly interpretation of biblical passages is indeed preoccupied with the Bible, but the modern methods of interpretation that such a scholar employs are so remote in spirit from the Bible that what this kind of scholar gets out of the Bible is something very different from the biblical view of life and the world. It often owes more to Kant, Hegel, or Heidegger than to Jeremiah or St. Paul.

Teilhard, like so many Frenchmen, was quite untouched by the influence of German philosophy and he is perhaps to us the supremely un-Hegelian man. He is so totally un-Hegelian in the entire cast of his thought that he never even bothers to be anti-Hegelian. Certainly in this teutonic sense of the term theologian, Teilhard is not a theologian.

Then, of course, there are those for whom theology is primarily a reconstruction of some kind of orthodoxy that employs the method of historical research. Earlier in this century the historians of the Catholic west specialized in mediaeval, or, as they usually preferred to call them, scholastic studies. Now the center of theological gravity has moved to the patristic age, and we are treated to lengthy historical essays delineating the views of this or that Greek or Latin Father. But if the theologian is supposed to be a kind of historian, then that fits Teilhard no better than the idea of the theologian as an erudite biblical scholar.

Teilhard was neither a historian of Christian thought nor an interpreter of the scriptures. Yet just as quite often Teilhard showed a better sense of the realism of scripture than the biblical scholars, so also in many departments of thought he is better equipped to interpret realistically the fathers and the scholastics more faithfully than many of the historians. This for very similar reasons.

Teilhard's love of the earth and the world saved him, unlike so many of his religious and theological contemporaries, from philosophical idealism. Like the bible and historic Christian thought, he is always a philosophical realist, and because of this he has an affinity with the Bible and historic Christian thought that is often lacking in biblical scholars and historians.

TEILHARD AND THEOLOGICAL DIALOGUE

If to be a theologian, however, is to contribute significantly to theological dialogue and renewal in one's own time, then Teil-

hard was a theologian indeed. Teilhard has laid the foundations of theological renewal in the twenty-first century, the century perhaps to which he truly belongs.

The twentieth century is witnessing the death of what the eigthteenth century began. In our time we behold the petering out of the "enlightenment" and, in response to the pressure of automation and technological advance, the gradual recession of the tidal wave of the industrial revolution as the age of leisure advances upon us. One of the reasons why people like Medawar disliked Teilhard so intensely is that he will insist on putting together things which the eighteenth century enlightenment insisted on putting asunder.

Teilhard, we may say, is the herald of the ultimate convergence of science and mysticism. Too often the hackneyed science and religion conflict turns out to be barren discussion between the second-hand science of popular scientific survey courses, and the second-hand religiousity of a merely institutional church. The spirit of first hand creative scientific research and first hand creative mystical faith experience are hardly ever engaged in the controversy.

Teilhard takes us into a deeper dimension. He is both researching and creative scientist and a praying Christian man, and he is struck and delighted by the close analogy and affinity that exists between the two. He is glad and surprised at the unlooked for experience of his unexpected integrity.

TEILHARD AND DANTE

I began this paper with Dante and the *Divine Comedy,* partly because I think that Teilhard is in his own way a poet. Not of course that he spent his time writing poetry but rather that he often succeeded in making poetry out of what appeared at first sight to be the most unpromising poetic materials. Above all, Teilhard had the poet's sense of the universality and significance of analogy, and even the intellectual poet's gift for perceiving what Plato saw so clearly centuries ago, the extraordinary kinship between conceptual and perceptual experiences.

A friend of mine who spent a whole day in a boat with Teilhard investigating rocks in Bartlett Sound, Mount Desert Island, Maine — in, I think, 1951, remarked that Teilhard seemed to perceive what most geologists merely conceive. Conversely he possessed the mystic's gift of seeming to conceive what most men suppose themselves to perceive.

But I have another reason altogether for comparing Teilhard to Dante. For Dante treats the Ptolomaic astronomy very much as Teilhard treated evolution. Just as Dante succeeded in expressing the whole drama of Christian existence in Ptolemaic terms, so Teilhard tried to express it in what are, rather loosely, called Darwinian terms. Of course we do not now in our days think of the *Divine Comedy* as a contribution to the science versus religious discussion, probably because Dante was within about a century of the Copernican revolution against the Ptolomaic astronomy. Dante we may say celebrated what turned out to be Ptolomy's funeral rites. He came to bury Caesar rather than to praise him. We have certainly no ground for supposing that the currents of thought in our culture set going by Darwin are anything like as close to their demise.

Again and again the supreme theological problem, in Dante's time as in ours, is that of re-mythologization. How are we to find in the prevailing secular culture a set of words and ideas in terms of which the gospel drama of faith and salvation can be vividly set forth, and so realistically that genuine communication will occur. In Dante's time all educated people, and even most practical people, such as navigators, for example, had accepted Ptolomy's astronomy for a millenium; but it was Dante who endeavored to show how perfectly it fitted the Christian scheme of salvation, and

42

how well the drama of Christian existence could be expressed in terms of it.

In Teilhard, in the same way, what some of the biblical theologians have called "sacred history" — meaning by "sacred history" at worst just the prophetic part of Hebrew history or, at best, Hebrew history in general, plus church history in general — is identified with the evolutionary history of the entire cosmos. For him there is nothing but sacred history, implying that there is no merely secular history, so that one more unsightly dualism that blemishes and impedes theological thought is put away.

TEILHARD'S THEOLOGICAL SOURCES

Yet, although Teilhard was not a theologian in the specialized biblical or historical sense, he had after all received a thorough theological training and it would perhaps be of interest to put together the elements drawn from the Bible or traditional Christian thought which particularly influenced him. Teilhard is one of that small select company of people who realized almost intuitively the vast and profound sense in which Christian orthodoxy from the beginning is longing, without knowing it, for a doctrine of evolution. So that when Darwin came he also without knowing it, initiated a new movement of thought that perfectly fitted the needs of the Christian theologian.

In the first place the account of the universe which we find in the fathers and the so-called scholastics conceives it as a structured hierarchy, which is only credible if it was created by evolution. The process of evolution, in which one dimension or level of being after another emerges out of and becomes the dominant characteristic of all that went before it makes sense of hierarchy. Hierarchy without evolution makes very little sense.

This is so far true that some fundamentalists like the Victorian geologist Gosse, have even supposed that God created the world in BC 4004 with all the evidence of an evolutionary process

that never took place already provided, presumably in order to humiliate the intellectual pride of self-confident biologists. Even for Gosse the world considered as a contemporary phenomenon looks like a world that has been created by evolution. Of course he does not believe that evolution ever happened, after all if the world was really created in BC 4004, there cannot have been any evolution, because there has not been enough time.

It is this lack of time which lead the ancients, the mediaevals and the early moderns to reject speculative ideas of evolution, which were always hanging about on the periphery of western intellectual culture. There is quite considerable evidence that many of them regarded some sort of evolutionary process as an attractive idea, — particularly St. Augustine and St. Thomas Aquinas — but they put it aside probably because of the fundamental difficulty that evolution demands more time than seemed to them at our disposal.

But the germ of later evolutionary ideas is more widespread in the theological tradition than merely the notion of hierarchy. There is, for example, in St. Paul and Origen the doctrine of "re-capitulation." This certainly seems to suggest the general idea of a later emergent that sums up and recapitulates the salient charac-teristics of its predecessors in the process out of which it emerged.

We may compare with this the doctrine of deification so strikingly important in the Greek fathers. The doctrine of deifica-tion does not mean, of course, that man ever becomes God, but it does mean that the Christian, through his unity with Christ in the Church and the Sacraments, shares or participates in Christ's unity with his Father, the unity, that is of the Persons of the Trinity. Loving and beloved the deified man will become saturated and glorious with Godhead.

The doctrine of deification cannot but suggest that whether or not we have a process of evolutionary change behind us, we certainly have many such drastic changes ahead of us. We may compare the doctrine of deification, as we find it in the Greek fathers, with Neitzsche's revolutionary doctrine of the superman, and with Samuel Alexander's prediction that the next stage in our evolution will be the emergence of a new dimension level of existence which very significantly he termed deity.

In the middle ages we encounter the significant debate about the plurality of forms. On the whole the Augustinians preferred this doctrine to that of the unicity of the form favored by Aquinas. For one thing a doctrine of the plurality of forms squared much better with the Christology of the council of Chalcedon. St. Thomas' contemporary at Paris, St. Bonaventure, even speaks of the lower form as "having its arms stretched out to embrace the higher," a phrase very close to evolution indeed.

Hierarchy, recapitulation, deification, the plurality of forms. All these traditional Christian notions in the imagination of Teilhard converge together into his more elaborate doctrine of cosmogenesis.

Other elements in the tradition that profoundly impressed him were the doctrine of the Trinity, with its idea of a concrete unity in love, which does not annual or destroy the persons entering into the unity, but rather reinforces and under-girds their individuality, and the doctrine of the hypostatic union, according to which Christ the God-man is quite literally divine without ceasing in any way to be totally human.

Teilhard's Incomplete Vision

In turning from this theme of Teilhard's theological sources to that of his contributions to the progress and renewal of contemporary theology, we must remind ourselves that the works of Teilhard are not finished or accomplished achievements. They are more like a stimulating agenda than a labor of love that has been brought to a successful conclusion. Teilhard would never have cried out "Consummatum est". It is this perhaps above all that

46

makes him so exciting to read. The writer is still so far from the perfection of his own vision that he leaves almost as much for the reader to do as he himself accomplished. This means that Teilhard cannot usefully be studied with the pedantry of the literary or historical scholar who delights to cite chapter and verse and who best expresses his expertise in a profusion of learned and accurate footnotes.

The student of Teilhard requires the intuitive gifts that enable him to discern not merely what Teilhard did think and say but also what he did not say but might very well have said under different circumstances. Using his methods, and to some extent even employing his terminology, our duty towards him is to carry his thought towards the ultimate destination rather than merely to quote and repeat what he actually wrote. This is, of course, always true. Teilhard does not require devoted Teilhardians who will overlay him and destroy his reputation as the Thomists came near to destroying Aquinas. In the twentieth century the Freudians have done much the same sort of thing with Freud. "Thank God I'm not a Marxist," said Karl Marx after listening to a boring speech at the First International.

We must beware of setting up a situation in which Teilhard might cry out, "Thank God I am not a Teilhardian". Nevertheless we can perhaps arrange Teilhard's chief contributions to contemporary theology under a series of appropriate headings:

TEILHARD AND NATURAL THEOLOGY

During most of the twentieth century natural theology has usually been regarded as a series of classical propositions and arguments that have been refuted once and for all by people like Hume and Kant. The reigning spirit in German theology at least professed to be rather pleased about this refutation, and natural theology was rejected altogether. It means that in practice theologians confined themselves to biblical and confessional theology and

altogether abdicated their apologetic responsibilities. Obviously biblical theology has nothing to say to the man who does not in some sense accept the authority of the Bible. The real question is whether natural theology is the name of a completed classical accomplishment that has unfortunately outlived its usefulness, or the name of a perennial intellectual quest, so that if one approach will not do, it is incumbent on us to try another.

Teilhard attempted to begin natural theology all over again and work towards a new natural theology for the Darwinian age. Much of the time he seemed to be feeling after an interpretation of Christian orthodoxy in evolutionary terminology. Such a project calls for one adventurous semantic experiment after another.

Teilhard was not always successful. For example, his attempts to provide a satisfactory doctrine of original and actual sin in his evolutionary terminology is by common consent less successful than some of his other ventures, but if we really believe in his methods this simply means that the Teilhardian doctrine of sin is still to be formulated. It may even remain on the theological agenda for decades.

Nevertheless perhaps at no point is Teilhard so significant for the theologian as in his new approach to natural theology. He has not only motivated us, but even enabled us to begin the whole work of natural theology and communicative apologetics all over again. When enthusiasts hail Teilhard as the new Aquinas this perhaps is what they have chiefly in mind.

TEILHARD AND NATURAL LAW

I will be brief here, but once more Teilhard's contribution to natural law is of the utmost importance. The classical doctrine of natural law, as we find it for example in Aquinas, is a left-wing or revolutionary doctrine. Too often when it is cited nowadays the concept of natural law is represented as a right wing or even reactionary doctrine that is hostile to novelty, development and change. Teilhard saw clearly, though I cannot recollect that he expressly states, that development, change and the emergence of novelty are by natural law characteristic of a creation whose Creator creates by evolution. All things change by natural law, and theology and ethics must be relevant to a series of changing contexts.

TEILHARD AND CHRISTOLOGY

Like most twentieth century thinkers and unlike the theological modernists of the nineteenth century, Teilhard's work calls for a heightened and intensified rather than a reduced Christology.

Normally, in the teutonic type of biblical theology the central Christological question is formulated as follows: "Is Jesus of Nazareth, or the Jesus of History, the Christ of Faith?" This way of putting the question at least makes sense when we suppose that Jesus of Nazareth, or the Jesus of History, is a clear figure on the historical horizon who can be lucidly and vividly presented by the historians. All that then remained to be done was to search in the words and actions of the reconstructed Jesus of History for some evidence that even in His own mind, He really was the Christ of Faith.

When, however, as in Rudolph Bultmann and others, the Jesus of History became if anything an even vaguer and more remote figure than the Christ of Faith, the time had perhaps come when the question should perhaps be asked the other way round.

Teilhard, of course, was in no sense replying to people like Bultmann and Gogarten. Almost certainly he had no opportunity of reading them, and we may surmise that he would not have bothered or even been interested if he had enjoyed the opportunity. Yet the Christological question in Teilhard does seem to present itself to his mind in the converse form. In the prologue to the Fourth Gospel it is the Word that is made flesh not the flesh that is made Word, and in Teilhard the question is never whether or not the Jesus of History is the Christ of Faith, but rather whether the Cosmic Christ, well-known to all of us whether we are Christians or not, the Cosmic Christ we may say *alias* the Old Testament Wisdom, *alias* the Platonic and Stoic Logos, *alias* nature, *alias* evolution, *alias* the *elan vital, alias* the dialectic of history is Jesus of Nazareth or the Jesus of History.

Teilhard, of course, never wrote a treatise on Christology, but the direction of his mind on this issue is reasonably clear. The Christ of Faith or cosmic Christ is the implicit Lord grasped in his universality. Jesus of Nazareth is the explicit Christ directly manifested in his particularity. Thus the Christological question is concerned with the particularity of the universal, whether this universal has a particularity and where that particularity is to be found.

As so often happens, philosophy and the Bible moving in their different orbits converge on the same ultimate questions. The precise modality of the particularity of a universal might be called a platonic question; the precise modality of a particular's universality is a biblical and existential question.

Just recently I was expounding this precise point to a class of seniors on the very verge of quitting this institution. One of the most intelligent of them said to me after the lecture, "If Teilhard is anything like right then most of what I have heard on this matter during my theological training has been wrong". I told him that he must take very seriously the possibility that this might indeed be so!

TEILHARD AND ESCHATOLOGY

What makes the eschatological passages in the Bible, and particularly in the New Testament, so incredible to most people is the old habit of trying to interpret them against a merely historical time scale. But of course the ancient world had no other time scale at its disposal. For the ancients, the world had been

created comparatively recently, and it was not difficult to suppose that it might end very shortly. The important thing was to insist that we are located in the middle of history, poised upon its great divide.

Teilhard makes it possible to think and preach eschatologically again by what seems in retrospect the simple device of interpreting these eschatological passages from the point of view not of a historical but of an evolutionary time scale. The emphasis of evolution up to the Incarnation has been on the emergence of a greater and richer profusion of variety. Since the incarnation the direction of evolution has shifted, or at least been deflected, towards the convergence of variety into a richer unity.

Defacto empirical men in the world can still find that theirs is the great period of transition, that their Christian duty is to stop looking backward and to start looking forward to that glorious future which the Creator who creates by evolution is determined upon and will surely bring to pass. Eschatology means that we stand in the middle way and that the future means more to us than the past.

TEILHARD AND BONHOEFFER

The twentieth century has not perhaps been rich in theological talent although there have, of course, been great twentieth century theologians. Karl Barth and Karl Rahner are perhaps the names that occur most readily to the mind. On the whole, however theology is not an area into which twentieth century genius characteristically pours its energies. Perhaps the only other significant theological figure whose name can be mentioned in the same breath as Teilhard de Chardin's is that of Dietrich Bonhoeffer.

Of course the two men were very different both in background and temperament. Teilhard was 26 when Bonhoeffer was born and he still had ten years to live when Bonhoeffer was hanged.

The German Bonhoeffer grew up in an educated, even academic type of household whose prevailing attitudes were more or less agnostic.

Teilhard, the Frenchman, sprang from a tradition that was aristocratic rather than professional and academic; and he imbibed the profound, at least semi-mystical, piety that never left him at his mother's knee. Bonhoeffer himself was theologically a disciple of Karl Barth and religiously a German Lutheran of almost the pietistic kind. Both were mystics, although both, for different reasons, might have resisted the word.

Teilhard was a faithful son of the Roman church who might have adapted to his own needs a quotation from Job: "Though it slays me yet I will trust in it." His attitude of patient, suffering love towards the Roman Church reminds us somewhat of Dr. Zhivago's love-hate relationship with Russia.

Yet different as these two men were and far removed as their backgrounds are from each other, somehow both got around to asking the same question. Bonhoeffer in a Nazi prison and Teilhard in the Gobi desert experienced the abandonment and dereliction of the Christian man who finds himself deprived of the ministry of the Word and the Sacraments in the fellowship of the Christian Church. Both found that even apart from the Church the life of faith can continue.

This is the basis of the new approach to the problems of natural theology so characteristic of them. Is it possible to find in the world forms of experience parallel to and supplementing the experience of God and Christ that we find in the Church? Both Bonhoeffer and Teilhard answered this question affirmatively, although they necessarily answered it each in a different way. Bonhoeffer meant by the world primarily the world of men and affairs. It was through participating in this world and suffering at its hands that Bonhoeffer found his unity with Christ on the cross. What Teilhard shares with Christ is not so much the physical passion on

Calvary as the Agony in the Garden on the previous night. For Teilhard the world is primarily the whole physical world of God's creation, and apparently from his boyhood onwards he had no difficulty about discerning God and Christ in the French countryside.

The extraordinary thing is not so much that two men so different answered their questions in different ways, but rather that they both asked the same question. Whether Teilhard and Bonhoeffer are the two greatest theological minds in the twentieth century is not perhaps the kind of question worth discussing, or even worth asking, but that they were the two most significant theological minds of our times seems to be so obvious as to brook no denial.

Yet Teilhard has a smack of permanence about him that Bonhoeffer lacks. Bonhoeffer is a child of the tormented twentieth century. Already I think he is becoming somewhat *passe* in the eyes of a generation that can remember neither the Nazi horror or the Second World War, a generation more concerned with getting to the moon than escaping the clutches of Facist tyranny. Teilhard exemplifies the very spirit of theological renewal. It is he perhaps who has laid the enduring foundations of the theology of a reunited and revivified church in the twenty-first century.

TEILHARD AND THEOLOGICAL RENEWAL

"Theological renewal" is, of course, another one of these cliches that have become so nauseatingly familiar in theological circles during the last twenty years. Renewal dialogue, situation ethics, professional training for the ministry, experience, event, acceptance, words and phrases like this are either unusable already or in a fair way to becoming unusable very shortly.

What does "theological renewal" really mean? I suggest that what we need in the Church today is some brilliant reminder that the theological enterprise and adventure are still going on, that we can see still around us evidence of novelty and growth com-

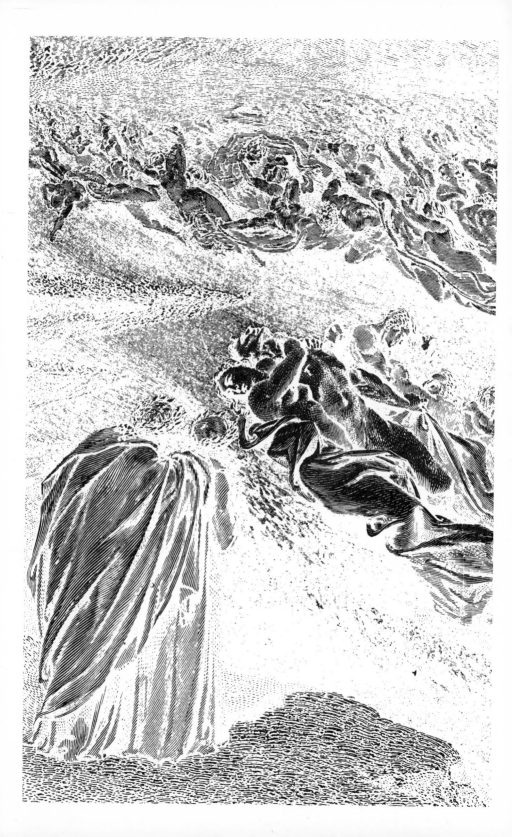

bined with complementary evidences of majestic continuity. The process which Newman called the "development of doctrine" must still be going on if living men are to find their life work in the thrilling adventure of theological thought.

I am a theologian myself, and nothing paralyzes me with horror so much as a concept of Christian orthodoxy that interprets it as something to be dredged up from the past by biblical scholars and historians. For me orthodoxy is an eschatological idea. All theology is oriented towards it, yet no theological formulation finally attains or comprehends it. The development of theology is like evolution, it is a coinherence of continuity and novelty.

The really exciting service that reading Teilhard's writings has done for me is to make me more vividly aware than I have ever been before that theology is still alive, that theology is still going on. For tradition does not mean a dead thing that is handed on by dying pedants, but rather a living thing that insists on handing itself on in an endless variety of new forms through the living minds that it possesses and dominates.

The mind of the true theologian is rather like the tomb in the Garden of Joseph of Arimathea. For it is there that the tradition rises again and again from the dead. Teilhard's mind was of this miraculous kind. When I first glanced at it I noticed only that the tomb was empty, but when I looked again I perceived with awe that the stone that separates modern man from mystery has been taken away.

Teilhard de Chardin
As Philosopher of History
By ROBERT V. WILSHIRE

INTRODUCTION

TEILHARD DE CHARDIN is one of the formative thinkers of our
time. He is the path blazer of what in the future must be a
continuing theological task, that is, the exploration of the theological significance of advances in knowledge by the physical
sciences. Nevertheless, I do not believe the case Teilhard presents
is beyond criticism. I do not think, for instance, that *The Phenomenon of Man* is a purely scientific treatise because Teilhard introduces non-scientific factors into his analysis. Indeed, I consider his
concept of "radial energy" an example of this.

Furthermore, I do not think that some of his conclusions
follow necessarily in terms of his own analysis. How can we allow

Teilhard's identification of Christ and Omega on any but metaphysical grounds?

Also, it could well be asked, "Why should there be point Omega at all, rather than point Sigma, just another phase in the unending process of evolution?" "Why should there be an end at all?" Teilhard's answer to this would point to the ascent of consciousness as in itself indicating a supreme level of consciousness toward which man is evolving, and this is what both guarantees direction, and the promise of fulfillment to the life of man and the cosmos as a whole.

Clearly Teilhard opted for Omega rather than Sigma because of the optimism that is the indelible mark of his Christian faith, and not as a result of strict scientific conclusions. For Teilhard Christianity is true, and as true, promises the end of all things in the conscious future of man, as man now understands consciousness. Teilhard is quite happy to admit, in his own words:

> "In short, this pole Omega is reached only by extrapolation; it remains by nature an assumption and a conjecture."
> When we accept "the evidence that the Christ of revelation is identical with the Omega of evolution," then "a way out begins to shine through the most distant future. In a world certainly open at its summit *in Christo Jesu,* we no longer risk dying of suffocation![1]

Given the sort of problems that the preceding examples point up, how best can we view Teilhard's critical and criticized position in the world of modern thought?

It is the intention of this paper to attempt to present a new perspective from which to approach Teilhard's phenomenological analysis of man in the cosmos; a perspective other than that of the narrow descriptive outlook of normal science which underlies most of the criticism directed at Teilhard. Of necessity this will bring us openly and unapologetically into the field of metaphysics. In other words, we will overtly admit to our consideration that

60

which Teilhard did not succeed in excluding. This, I trust, will reveal a richer dimension to his theories, and the true implications of his work.

The groundwork for this angle of approach I have borrowed from Hans Jonas who seeks in his book *The Phenomenon of Life* to lay a foundation for a philosophical anthropology.

The latter part of my paper follows this up with a further connection with the philosophical theology of Paul Tillich with a particular reference to his presentation of myth and symbol.

BEYOND THE SCIENTIFIC METHOD: A SEARCH FOR MEANING

In developing his theme Jonas presents a fascinating study of the changes that have taken place in man's understanding of himself and the cosmos from primitive times. Early man in interpreting the nature of things, "and this he did when he began to be man,"[2] did so in terms of an elementary panpsychism which saw life in everything and had no real concept of the inanimate. However, the Copernican revolution, which we can see as a dramatic representative of the change of perspective necessitated by scientific method,

> . . . widened this horizon into the vastness of cosmic space [such that] the proportional place of life in the scheme of things [was] sufficiently dwarfed so that it became possible to disregard it for most of what henceforth was to be the content of the term "nature." But to early man, standing on his earth arched by the dome of its sky, it could never occur that life might be a side issue in the universe, and not its pervading rule.[3]

Till this time man's place in nature presented no insuperable difficulties. It was just one aspect of life within the total life of the world. The Copernican cosmos changed all this. The answer to the question, "What is the world like?" became much more complicated, leading to the emergence of the experimental scien-

tific method as offering the most satisfactory path to knowledge, and the philosophical separation of "mind" and "matter" as a necessary basis for this process, which was finally canonized in the Cartesian metaphysics of Descartes. It so cemented man in a dualism that he would never escape without once again going through a radical change in perspective.

Jonas presents an analysis of how this came about, and the part played in the process by the "tyranny and nobility of sight."[4] Of all the senses this is the most important. By sight man is able to stand back from the world and regard it apart from himself, and so establish a rigid subject-object relationship, a relationship which has been of such fundamental importance in the development of the physical sciences, but which has made man a stranger in an inanimate world of objects.

The primitive vitalistic monism that included man has been replaced by a mechanistic monism that has no place for him. Whereas death was the problem of pre-Cartesian man, which he dealt with by magic and doctrines of immortality, the problem of modern man is life, and the despair that follows from finding no natural place for it in the only world that science knows.

Examples of the philosophical expression of this problem are to be found in the skepticism of Hume, the nihilism of Nietzsche, the despair of so much existentiaist thinking, and the irrational subjectivist theories that enthrone feeling in the place of reason as the basis of belief, knowledge, and action. The idealism of Berkeley and the monadology of Leibnitz represents attempts to avoid the dualism set up by the Cartesian approach to knowledge, while the Kantian categories of the mind sought to reduce this dualism to its least offensive expression.

Science, in its pragmatic way, unconsciously followed a similar procedure to that of Kant, in attempting to limit one side of the dualism, that is, mind, to the least possible area, thus widening the scope of its own sovereignty to a maximum.[5] As Jonas says, while Berkeley and Leibnitz sided with the *res cogitans,*

> . . . natural science had no option in its choice of "matter." Much as science would like to have its choice understood in terms of method only and to be spared a *confessio fidei,* there are those among its own proper objects that force it to face the issue of materialism on the ontological level. These objects are living organisms, the mysterious meeting-place of Descartes' two substances, though he himself acknowledged such a "meeting" in only one case.[6]

Science had even made of man's body an object of knowledge, with the mind a disembodied, subjective knower, and by treating animals simply as bodies, thus left to man as his personal peculiarity the "inwardness" that separated him from the rest of nature and made all this latter available to a purely mechanical analysis. However, says Jonas, science defeated itself by its very success, for one of the products of that success was the theory of evolution,

> . . . and evolution precisely abolished the special position of man which had warranted the Cartesian treatment of all the remainder. The *continuity* of descent now established between man and the animal world made it impossible any longer to regard his mind, and mental phenomena as such, as the abrupt ingression of an ontologically foreign principle at just this point of the total flow. With the last citadel of dualism there also fell the isolation of man, and his own evidence became available again for the interpretation of that to which he belongs.[7]

The separation of mind and matter into two "substances" had made man a foreigner in the world. Evolution has made of him a citizen once again.

Certainly, this result of evolutionary thinking in the arena of science is not at once obvious at an empirical level. It *is* possible to think of evolution as a mechanical process, and a descriptive science determined not to examine its own metaphysical assumptions may well do so.

64

Jonas discusses this in his consideration of the "Philosophical Aspects of Darwinism"[8] in which he sees natural science pushing the stumbling block of spontaneous generation, with all its attendant problems associated with the theory of probability, into

> . . . the very first instance of life as such, where its magnitude and therefore its theoretical inconvenience are reduced in proportion to the minimum of organization assumed in these first beginnings. Immeasurably consequential as was the first step, the transition from inorganic to organic, it can hypothetically be made small enough not to overstrain the probabilities of chance combination. . . . The minimum left to the original essence of life is just self-preservation. . . . Mind was not foreseen in the amoeba, nor was the vertebrate structure, science no more than the opposable thumb; one and the other were elicited in due — but unforeseeable — course in the enormous span of the changing vital situation. The variability is essentially instability, which itself testifies to the absence of a predetermined substantial form. . . . Some initial conditions being different, the solar system would not exist or would be otherwise than it is, and the completeness of nature as an equilibrium-system would be none the worse for it. "Necessity plus contingency" can be most simply expressed here by saying that there is the complete concourse of *causes* but no *reason* for the system as it happens to exist.[9]

From this point of view,

> . . . the so-called "higher" structures may well emerge from more primitive ones *accidentally,* i.e., by the agency of entirely primitive forces. If higher levels happen to emerge in the dynamics of the primitive, their quality as levels is wholly contingent, though their factuality is necessary.[10]

Thus the growth in complexity of the organism leading to the higher animals and eventually to man could be seen as nothing but a meaningless monstrosity, the result of an original amoeba subject to a long history of disease, and the categories of "higher"

and "lower" forms of life are nothing but a "sport" thrown up by a directionless genetic process.

The perspective of descriptive science reveals man, therefore, as a "sport," and nothing more. Though modern research presents us with more and more data of the universe such that the total of our knowledge is ever increasing, at the same time it is ever widening the limits of the universe. We are aware of a more than compensating growth in areas of possible knowledge about which we know nothing.

Man is faced with a paradox: the more he knows, the more there is to know. He seems to have been thrown up by a physical universe which is prevented from laughing at his feeble attempts to find out what it is like only by the fact that the universe, in its inanimate deadness, knows nothing of him, including his thoughts about its own composition. Pascal expressed this rather well when he said: "Cast into the infinite immensity of spaces of which I am ignorant, and know me not, I am frightened."[11] But this is not all that man is aware of. Pascal also says:

> Man is only a reed; the feeblest reed in nature. But he is a *thinking* reed. There is no need for the entire universe to arm itself in order to annihilate him. A vapour, a drop of water suffices to kill him. But were the universe to crush him man would yet be more noble than that which slays him. Because man knows that he dies and understands the advantage that the universe has over him. Of this the universe knows nothing.[12]

Pascal has put his finger on the two facts that the descriptive method fails to take account of: "thought" and "nobility"; and in the theory of evolution both science and philosophy have been brought face to face with this fact. Thought is "more than" the activity of a disembodied mind. It is the product of the whole man, and is, therefore, "of the earth, earthy."[13] A dualism that fails to take account of this, useful as it may be in other ways for describing and understanding man's situation, must be prepared to leave the way open to an approach to knowledge that does take account of it, or opens the possibility of doing so. It is the exclusiveness of the claims of the method of descriptive science, and the dualism that lies behind it, that must be objected to as being inadequate, despite the influence that such claims have had in structuring the thinking of so much of modern society at all levels of intellectual accomplishment.

The scientific experimental method was the practical development that resulted from man's attempt to answer the question: "What is the world like?" and in framing its point of reference, and way of attacking the problem, it did so from a particular ontological perspective. We could call this the *myth of objectification*. As such it helped man to see the world more clearly, and of much more importance, it made him really aware of what he was himself.

By standing back from nature man was no longer lost in it. It became something that he could study, use, and eventually manipulate to fulfill his own needs, and in the process man experienced one aspect of transcendence, the superiority of the animate to the inanimate, of the thinking over that which can never "know." Man's separate existence as one side of a dualism resulted in his own history, peculiar to himself.

But there is still a something "more" to man's awareness of transcendence that is not accounted for by descriptive method.[14] There is another question that can be asked apart from "What is the world like?", and that is, "What does the world mean?"

As questions they are equally legitimate. The first may have the appearance of being more fundamental; but this is simply because it appears to be more scientific. However, as we have seen, the method that was developed to answer it has behind it its own assumptions, its own ontology, its own myth. Its apparently more secure ground as a question to which there is a real answer, or in some way more "real" than seems to be the case with our other question, is merely the consequence of the prejudice associated with the special quality of certainty that is popularly attached to a particular limited view of science.

Technically, descriptive science is not equipped to answer questions of meaning and value, though by default it often appears to do so.[15] Again, this is largely the result of popular confidence in science and its ability to answer questions. The traditional methods of answering such questions are those of philosophy and theology; but these have fallen on evil days precisely because of the advantage with respect to certainty that natural science apparently has over them.

To answer the limited questions of value and meaning that our present age seems interested in asking, science is forced, though not openly, to adjust its ontological perspective. Just one illustration of this is to be seen in the ease with which an "is" is often confused with an "ought." For example no one can deny the influence that the Kinsey Report has had on the morality of our generation; and much of this is the result of the assumption that a description of what man's actual behavior "is" describes what it "ought" to be. Indeed, in some instances, perhaps many, this may well be the case. But it is an assumption that cannot be made without raising questions with which descriptive science, in terms of the experimental method, and its particular philosophical assumptions, is not equipped to deal.

Much of the confusion as to what is properly to be regarded as science arises from this tendency of science to broaden its horizons to take account of factors other than that which merely "is." This is particularly understandable in a world where man is increasingly becoming able to determine aspects of future development through his powers over nature, and hence, environment, that science and its allied function, technology, are making available. In an important sense, the future will be partially, at least, man's creation.

Obviously, the vast range of choices facing man as a consequence of this are known to scientists long before they are known to philosophers and theologians. As a result, the future we are currently creating by the activity of the present risks being the product of those whose value judgments are the result of practical rules-of-thumb, or such philosophically vague concepts as "the common good," or the "most happiness for the most people" which the Utilitarians of the last century developed, and which, in this, have become the watchwords of political action. Perhaps, of even greater importance, in the creation of the future, will be the maxims of business and commerce, the profit motive, and the market machinery balancing supply and demand. It would seem to me that none of this does justice to the "nobility" of man that Pascal pointed to, or to man's sense of transcendence.

Quite clearly, a dynamic science cannot be content to describe what "is" when at the same time it is creating the future, and in the process raising the question "where do we go from here?" This in turn brings with it questions of meaning, direction, and ultimacy. The time is overdue for a radical exposure of the ontological assumptions underlying our science dominated way of life. The question "what does the world mean?" deserves to be taken seriously once more. It is a very "real" question indeed!

Jonas is convinced that this question must be faced. An adequate philosophy of life "must deal with the organic facts of life, and also with the self-interpretation of life in man. It must interpret both."[16] However, though this must lead to the removal of a hard and fast departmentalization between science, philosophy, and theology in coming to grips with the problem, some sort of distinction must be maintained between a *de facto* account of phenomena and the attempt to uncover meaning in it. Heidegger's "ontic" inquiry, and the "signification" of Sartre would seem to be appropriate categories. Jonas is aware of the importance of this distinction. In no way is he guilty, as is Teilhard, of making a

71

category of "signification" an essential part of the "ontic" description. He does not threaten scientists with metaphysical concepts which they feel should show up in their microscopes.

The *myth of objectification* that underlies the experimental method of descriptive science is inadequate by itself to give a full account of man's experience of himself and his situation. However, an allied *myth of being* may well do so by raising the question of meaning and allowing man the sense of transcendence as being significant, by which he can transcend the dualism of the myth of objectification, and the despair associated with it. Yet a myth of being, offering as it does the possibility of man understanding himself, must be more embracing than the myth of objectification to the extent that it must also take account of the latter.

One link in the connection between the two myths is to be found in "evolution," for it is this theory that, above all, exposes the inadequacy of materialism, and the myth on which it is based. As Jonas says:

> So it happened that in the hour of the final triumph of materialism, the very instrument of it, "evolution," implicitly transcends the terms of materialism and posed the ontological question anew — when it seemed settled. And Darwinism, more than any other doctrine responsible for the now dominant evolutionary vision of all reality, turns out to have been a thoroughly dialectical event. This becomes increasingly visible as its teachings are philosophically assimilated. Whatever their success so far, all contemporary revisions of traditional ontology indeed start, almost axiomatically, from the concept of being as *becoming,* and in the phenomenon of cosmic evolution look for a key to a possible stand beyond the old alternatives.[17]

Our new myth must be in some sense, therefore, *a myth of being as becoming.* In fact, while Jonas does not use such terms as the myth of objectification and the myth of being as becoming, he does suggest that the appropriate way to express awareness of transcendence is in a myth which takes account of it, for

> Myth taken *literally* is crudest objectification.
> Myth taken *allegorically* is sophisticated objectification.
> Myth taken *symbolically* is the glass through which we darkly see.[18]

Jonas sees no significant connection between his work and that of Teilhard de Chardin. He has only two references to Teilhard in *The Phenomenon of Life,* and one of these is an unimportant footnote. The other is to be found in his Foreword when he says:

> The reader will . . . find nothing here of the evolutionary optimism of a Teilhard de Chardin, with life's sure and majestic march toward a sublime consummation. He will find life viewed as an experiment with mounting stakes and risks which in the fateful freedom of man may end in disaster as well as success. And the difference from de Chardin's as also from other, and better conceived, metaphysical success stories, will, I hope, be recognized as one not merely of temperament but of philosophical justice.[19]

Yet I think a connection can be made between them by adjusting Teilhard's metaphysical position in terms of Jonas' implied criticisms, that is, to maintain some distinction between the scientific account of phenomena and the attempt to uncover meaning in it. Also, there is an optimism to be found in Jonas. He really does seem to hold the hope that man can face the challenge of reconciling what he knows about himself and the world with that which he is always becoming. However, the tentative myth he suggests under the symbols[20] he selects fails to take the possibility of a concrete, phenomenological revelation seriously enough.

By failing to raise the questions that surround the person of Jesus of Nazareth, the one outstanding claim to such a revelation, he has unduly limited the scope of man's search for transcendence. Phenomenologically, an Incarnation is only romantic nonsense in

a situation in which it has not occurred. In which case it is at best, wishful thinking in terms of the possibilities of an infinitely open future, or misrepresentation of a past event. But where it has occurred, by providing more meaningful symbols, a myth of being not only opens up the possibility of transcendence, but also what that transcendence itself ultimately means.

A Myth For Our Times

We have suggested that there are grave difficulties from an empirical point of view associated with the Teilhardian analysis: that the enthusiastic and substantially uncritical acceptance of the synthesis he proposes, a feature of much modern literature on the subject, is unjustified. On the other hand, criticisms and condemnations, equally sweeping in scope, are just as unjustified. The polarization of so much opinion into opposing camps of supporters and detractors has added to the problem of attempting to strike a balanced appreciation.

While it would seem that a substantial case can be made for his basic methodological approach, there remains, in terms of that approach, a considerable area in which conclusions other than, and incompatible with, Teilhard's own, can be drawn. The particular factors concerned, leading to such various conclusions, center on aspects of Teilhard's analysis which are not themselves subject to verification. Individuals will accept or reject Teilhard's proposed synthesis, in whole or in part, in terms of how far it is compatible with such facts as are verifiable, and also with whatever other theories and beliefs are held which interpret the "ontic" world and allow it "signification."

One of the major problems of Teilhard's approach is that at times he does seem to be claiming a "straight empirical road through nature to God."[21] This would appear to be the implication of describing *The Phenomenon of Man* as purely a scientific treatise. Even in this the most scientific of Teilhard's theologics-philosophical writings, he interpolates extra-scientific considerations into the analysis, in order to draw his conclusions. In other words, he does not really argue directly from descriptive biology to God in purely scientific terms. In fact, any scientific theory relating to the existence of God and his activity, to be truly and exclusively scientific in the narrow sense of the word, must be open to the sort of verification at a phenomenological level as would have the result of removing the existence of God from any real possibility of doubt. Such certitude would have very grave consequences for the Christian doctrines of God and man.[22]

The traditional attempts to prove the existence of God share this same problem. To be acceptable as "proofs" they must display a logical or demonstrable character so thorough as to lead to only one possible conclusion. A God so obvious to man would in no way be able to be denied. He would dominate man's awareness in such a way as to deny his freedom. Man would be a creature of far less significance than his self-awareness discloses. The only alternative that would allow a demonstrable God, always subject to the demands of human logic and science, and their respective principles of verification, would be a God little removed from the genie of Aladdin's lamp; a finite God under the control of man, having no connection with the God man has experienced in history.

The very richness of the Christian understanding of God and man depends on the fact that "now we see through a glass darkly,"[23] and then only with the eyes of faith. This is the necessary condition for the truly human situation. Only so can man be free to respond with love to love. Only so can love itself have meaning.

Teilhard has attempted the important task of relating the particular "signification" of the world and the universe that is to be found in the Christian faith with the empirical facts as science has uncovered them. In fact, if truth is a unity, and it makes no sense if it is not, then these should indeed be compatible.[24] At certain points in his theory Teilhard has imputed to particular factors in his scientific description tendencies or characteristics which are insights of faith rather than actual products of the empirical investigation of phenomena. As such, once this extra-scientific point has been reached, they are no longer subject to the procedures of scientific verification. This is a valid practice provided it is clear what precisely is being done and provided that established empirical facts are not violated in the process. Areas of incompatibility would indicate either faulty science or poor insights of faith, and criticisms in these terms would be thoroughly justified.

Much of the confusion and differing opinion associated with Teilhard's approach results from his own failure to distinguish clearly the meeting ground between his empirical science and his faith. We may, perhaps, excuse this to some extent by seeing much of this confusion as the deliberate result of his difficulties in getting his works published. While he was permitted to publish his scientific work he was under strict obedience not to publish his theological views, as these were considered by authorities in Rome as being of an unorthodox nature. He modified *The Phenomenon of Man* many times in an attempt to obtain permission to publish. It is understandable that he would attempt to present as science as wide an area of his ideas as possible.

From a solely empirical perspective we have already noted important limitations of the Teilhardian synthesis. Having now acknowledged non-verifiable elements in his analysis, it remains to be seen if it is possible to find a non-empirical approach to his thought that will have the result of opening up metaphysical insights which sat uneasily in his theories when seen from the purely scientific viewpoint.

The sort of thing that Teilhard has attempted is not new. There have been many attempts to establish such a synthesis between religion and science. One of the most important and long-lived of these is, of course, to be found in the book of Genesis in the Old Testament. A similar process can be noted in other cul-

tures, as in the Vedic writing of the post-Aryan invasion period in India.[25]

Such a process seems to be provoked when a particular faith or vehicle of "signification" of the human situation comes in contact with a scientific understanding of the world that is in some way more advanced than that in which the faith had previously been expressed. This is the situation that led to re-presentation of the Israelite religion in terms of the Babylonian science.[26]

Today we refer to the result as a creation myth. This is not to say that we find no value in the account of creation to be found in the first book of Genesis. It still finds significant interpretation in theological writings in which it is demythologized in both scientific and theological terms. The science of this particular myth, in modern times, has generally been discarded as being no longer relevant, but the theological insights have been adapted and moulded to the further insights of the Old Testament and Christian experience. In a sense, they are "remythologized." We can see this as a continuing process. For example, the doctrine of "Original Sin" has been subject to much rethinking, that is, remythologizing, in recent times.[27] However, by and large, the biblical creation myth has not been replaced by a modern myth that takes into account man's increased knowledge of the physical universe. Hence our traditional myth, and creation, seem to have little bearing on one another.

The old science-religion controversy of the last century has lingered on into this century such that a gap of increasing proportions has developed between the two approaches to truth. It is my contention that we can make the most sense of Teilhard's synthesis if we see it essentially as a new creation myth attempting to bridge that gap.

I should make clear that I am not claiming that Teilhard intended to create such a myth. In regarding it as such we are changing his stated perspective to what I consider to be the most useful perspective to adopt in evaluating his actual achievement.

We are not seeking to find God as a corollary to empirical biology and allied sciences, but rather to view these latter from the insights of Christian faith. In effect this is in fact what Teilhard did when he brought together the data of science and the data of revelation, with presumed metaphysical consequences that the empirical data could not support.

Our new viewpoint, not being subject to the limitations of the verification principle, has greater metaphysical possibilities, allowing such concepts as "radial energy" and a climactic "Omega point," and such identification as he makes between "Omega" and Jesus, if these will provide us with profounder insights into the Christian "signification" of the "ontic" world. While such factors in his theory as these may not fly in the face of empirical evidence, they are now freed from the necessity to be the product of it.

In Teilhard a theology expressed in terms of an outmoded science came face to face with a scientific approach that was obviously superior. His great achievement lies not so much in achieving a synthesis but in the fact that he attempted it. Already his science is out of date, and his theology was never that of a specialist theologian. His myth, therefore, must present its difficulties.

In a period of such acceleration in the rate of scientific discovery, the days have gone when such a synthesis will stand for a millennium or longer. However, Teilhard has succeeded in focusing attention on what must be in the future a constant theological task; a task that, of necessity, only a thinker versed in both science and theology can presume to undertake.

The very word "myth" has many problems associated with it. However, recent philosophical and theological analysis of the whole subject has rehabilitated myth as a respectable means of expressing matters of ultimate concern and value.[28] This is not to claim that a myth may say that which cannot be said.

While A. J. Ayre has adopted a far too rigid anti-metaphysical attitude in his *Language, Truth and Logic,* which attitude he modified substantially in the preface to the second edition, he is correct when he says that any form of statement, including myth, conveys nothing at all unless its content can be clearly exposed in logical terms.[29] Paul Tillich repeats this directly in relation to myth when he says: "Every myth contains a theological thought which can be, and often has been, made explicit." He goes on to say: "Priestly harmonizations of different myths sometimes disclose profound theological insights."[30]

In Teilhard's attempted synthesis we have a harmonization of myths drawn from science and theology. It is easy to see the mythological element in a science that is long out of date. But currently held scientific theory has about it an aura of empirical certitude that leads most casual observers to conclude that myth can be in no way a suitable vehicle to express what is being said. However, modern science is turning more openly to metaphorical, and therefore mythical, modes of expression, as mathematics proves inadequate to the task of stating what science understands to be true of our expanding universe. It remains to be seen what "profound theological insights" can be gained from the Teilhardian analysis.

Now I will endeavor to open up Teilhard's creation myth in terms of Tillich's own presentation of myth and symbol[31] and the role they play in Christian theology.

The theory of evolution takes history seriously, looking to the record written by nature herself for its basic evidence. Tillich sums up his analysis of history in his *Systematic Theology* thus:

> The aim of history can now be expressed in terms of the three processes of life and their unity in the following way: history, in terms of the self-integration of life, drives toward centeredness of all history — bearing groups and their individual members in an unambiguous harmony

of power and justice. History, in terms of the self-creativity of life drives toward the creation of a new, unambiguous state of things. And history, in terms of the self-transcendence of life, drives toward the universal, unambiguous fulfilment of the potentiality of being.

But history, like life in general, stands under the negatives of existence and under the ambiguities of life. The drive toward universal and total centeredness, newness, and fulfilment is a question and remains a question as long as there is history. This question is implied in the great ambiguities of history which have always been felt and powerfully expressed in myth, religious and secular literature, and art. They are the questions to which (in the sense of the method of correlation) the religious (and quasi-religious) interpretations of history as well as the eschatological symbolism relate. They are the questions to which, within the circle of Christian theology, the Kingdom of God is the answer.[32]

Tillich's "history-bearing" groups relate to modern man, i.e., *homosapiens*. However, Teilhard's evolutionary view of history regards all species within the evolutionary process as "history-bearing," and interprets "life" rather in the wider sense of the Bergsonian *elan-vital*.[33] However, Bergson's open-ended future is modified in Teilhard by what is in effect the Tillichian "centeredness" that is the consequence of the drive toward unambiguous fulfilment of being. Within these limitations it is clear that Teilhard and Tillich have much common ground.

In commenting on Bergson's thought, Tillich says:

The future is genuine only if it is open, if the new can happen and if it can be anticipated. This is the motive that led Bergson to insist upon the absolute openness of the future to the point of making God dependent on the unforeseen that might happen. But in teaching the absolute openness of the future, Bergson devalued the present by denying the possibility of its anticipation. A God who is not able to anticipate every possible future is dependent on an absolute accident and cannot be the foundation of an ultimate courage. This God would himself be subject to the anxiety of the unknown. He would not be being-itself. Therefore, a relative although not an absolute openness to the future is the characteristic of eternity. . . . Without the element of openness, history would be without creativity. It would cease to be history. On the other hand, without that which limits openness, history would be without direction. It would cease to be history.[34]

For Tillich that which limits openness is the eternal present *(nunc eternum),*[35] a symbol that views the present from the category of Eternal Life, is guaranteed by the Spirit of God, and actualized in the Kingdom of God.

Tillich states:

Religious symbolism has produced three main symbols for the unambiguous life: Spirit of God, Kingdom of God, and Eternal Life. . . . The Spirit of God is the presence of the Divine Life within creaturely life. The Divine Spirit is "God present." The Spirit of God is not a separated being. Therefore one can speak of "Spiritual Presence" in order to give the symbol its full meaning.

. . . The symbol "Spiritual Presence" uses the dimension of spirit, the bearer of which is man, but in order to be present in the human spirit, the Divine Spirit must be present in all the dimensions which are actual in man, and this means, in the universe.

The symbol Kingdom of God . . . embraces the destiny of the life of the universe, just as does the symbol "Spiritual Presence." But history's quality of running irreversibly toward a goal introduces another element into its symbolic meaning, and that is the "eschatological" expectation, the expectation of the fulfilment toward which self-transcendence strives and toward which history runs. Like Spiritual Presence, the Kingdom of God is working and struggling in history; but as eternal fulfilment of life, the Kingdom of God is above history. . . .

Spiritual Presence creates Eternal Life in those who are grasped by it. And the Kingdom of God is the fulfilment of temporal life in Eternal Life.[36]

Later Tillich says of the Kingdom of God that its connotations . . . are more embracing than those of the two others. This is a consequence of the double character of the Kingdom of God. It has an inner-historical and a transhistorical side. As inner-historical, it participates in the dynamics of history; as transhistorical, it answers the questions implied in the ambiguities of the dynamics of history. In the former quality it is manifest through the Spiritual Presence; in the latter it is identical with Eternal Life.[37]

It is clear that the principal symbol in Tillich's interpretation of history, which is itself an interpretation myth, is the Kingdom of God. By standing outside of history[38] it provides an aim, an end,[39] toward which the present is drawn. From within history it is a directive principal in association with the "finite freedom"[40] of man by which the ambiguities of our empirical life are transcended in the struggle toward fulfilment.[41] It is only within this symbol that a myth of history, and therefore history itself, becomes possible. Without it there can be no history, but merely a process that knows nothing of creativity or direction.

The parallels with Teilhard's concept of the Omega point, which also stands outside history, and, simultaneously, is active within it, need not be labored. In fact, Teilhard looks on the universe as "The Divine Milieu." The symbol of the Kingdom of God is the implicit perspective through which he comes to grips with the phenomenological universe, and it is precisely this that provokes the antagonism of those who would view it solely from the perspective of empirical science.

As we have seen earlier, both in terms of Teilhard's scientific methodology and the alternative construction of Hans Jonas, from such an empirical perspective, Teilhard's conclusions are in no way necessary. They are contingent on the "signification" that

85

results from approaching them under the symbol of the Kingdom of God. Empirically there is only *process.* Direction, progress,[42] levels[43] of being, and creation itself are all the insights of myth.

Tillich has given us a myth opening up creative history, and Teilhard, a myth opening up creative evolution (which is a particular way of looking at history). Both are creation myths; and, as such, they are myths of being. By taking evolution into account they are myths of being-as-becoming. Together they may well indicate the possible lines of development of a viable myth for our times. The metaphysical implications of such a myth would transcend the metaphysical limitations of descriptive science in much the same way as, through the myth, man transcends the ambiguities of his empirical life. As Tillich says: "Within the circle of Christian theology, the Kingdom of God is the answer," and as such it is "a most important and most difficult symbol of Christian thought."[44]

Both Teilhard and Tillich appreciate the centrality of the Incarnation to the Christian "signification," though neither seems very fond of the word itself. Tillich explicitly repudiates it, as being inadequate, and develops the theme in terms of the "logos" doctrine which lends a dynamic interpretation to what otherwise appears to be a single, static event. He sees the cosmic implications of the logos as "the bearer of the New Being . . . not only to save individuals and to transform man's historical existence but to renew the universe. And the assumption is that mankind and individual men are so dependent on the powers of the universe that salvation of the one without the other is unthinkable."[45]

However, Tillich does not seem able to drive his analysis to what appears to be its logical conclusion so that the Incarnation and the victory associated with it are available to the whole universe, but "restricts the expectation of the Christ to historical mankind" while leaving open the possibility of "singular incarnations for other unique worlds."[46] Eric Mascall comes to quite other conclusions, seeing the one Incarnation as applicable to all sentient beings, including those that may exist on other worlds.[47] Teilhard takes this even further, and in his theory of Christogenesis, developing Pauline theology,[48] identifies the converging center of the evolutionary universe with the central act of history, that is, the Christ event.[49] For him "the Christ of revelation is quite simply Omega."[50]

In Teilhard, then, we have an expanded form of the Tillichian theory of history, to take account more thoroughly of evolution, including under the symbol of Omega the symbol of the Kingdom of God and those associated with it by Tillich, i.e., Spiritual Presence and Eternal Life.

Nevertheless, Tillich does recognize the role of evolution, (though not thoroughly enough to satisfy Teilhard or Jonas) and reflects Teilhard's insistence on the importance of inwardness and centeredness but he cannot quite bring himself to apply such a directly psychological factor to the inanimate world in any explicit way, and attempts to leave open the question of the psychic element in non-human animal life, by referring to it as being merely potential. A solution

> . . . must be given for the problem of the transition from the dimension of the vegetative to that of the animal, especially to the phenomenon of an individuals "inner awareness" of himself. Here again the distinction of the potential from the actual provides the solution: potentially, self-awareness is present in every dimension; actually, it can appear only under the dimension of animal being. The attempt to pursue self-awareness back into the vegetative can be neither by intuitive participation or by reflexive analogy to expressions similar to those man finds in himself. Under these circumstances, it seems wiser to restrict the assumptions of inner awareness to those realms in which it can be made highly probable, at least in terms of analogy, and emotionally certain in terms of participation — most obviously in the higher animals.

Under special conditions the dimension of inner awareness, or the psychological realm, actualizes within itself another dimension, that of the personal-communal or the "spirit." Within reach of present human experience, this has happened only in man. The question of whether it has happened anywhere else in the universe cannot yet be answered positively or negatively.[51]

At a later stage Tillich goes on to say:

The higher animals do not transcend the satisfaction of their immediate needs; the animals do not transcend their natural bondage. Nor is there any particular intention operating in the evolution of the species or in the movement of the universe . . . there is no absolute meaning and there is no significant uniqueness where the dimension of the spirit is not actual. The uniqueness of a species or of a particular exemplar within a species is real but not ultimately significant, whereas the act in which a person establishes himself as a person, a cultural creation with its inexhaustible meaning, and religious experience in which ultimate meaning breaks through preliminary meaning are infinitely significant. These assertions are based on the fact that life under the dimension of the spirit is able to experience ultimacy and to produce embodiments and symbols of the ultimate.[52]

In fact, I am not at all sure that there is any real difference between Tillich's concept of "potential self-awareness present in every dimension," which includes the inanimate and animal creation, and Teilhard's "psychic or radial energy" when seen under the symbol of the Kingdom of God. Both see the cosmic implications of human life, the universe fulfilling itself and its potentialities through man, and only in man expressing its ultimate significance.

The word "potential" is a very useful one, but fraught with difficulties. In a sense, it would seem that whatever is potential is in some way actual in the potentiality. It may be objected to this, however, that an entirely open-ended future would make all devel-

opments possible, i.e., potential, but only one, or a limited combination, of these would become actual.[53] But, we have seen earlier that Tillich does not have the concept of an entirely open-ended future. Its openness is limited by creativity and direction, and this would also have been the case at any particular time in the past.

Evolution itself, even at an empirical level of study, and not subjected to "signification," is not entirely open-ended, though future possibilities at any one present time may be vast. The actuality of any particular present does, in fact, limit the openness of the potentiality of the future, by limiting the factors that may contribute to that future. Nevertheless, this limited openness of potentiality only becomes creative and directional under the symbol of the Kingdom of God. Only under such a symbol can potential or actual self-awareness on the part of the inanimate have any meaning.

Teilhard has merely added to Tillich's metaphor drawn from psychology an added factor borrowed from the empirical sciences. Essentially their function is the same. Teilhard's myth includes explicitly as history that which Tillich includes implicitly,[54] and which, because it is only implicit, to my mind, sits somewhat uneasily in his analysis. Only by widening the definition of history in this way can the ambiguities of "potential self-awareness," and therefore, presumably, potential history, be removed. (For Tillich history is possible only under conditions of actual human awareness, for only then can there be recognition of a predicament to be transcended.)[55]

It is difficult to see, for example, how merely "potential self-awareness," that is in no way actual, could be associated with, and in some sense guarantee, an evolutionary process of the order that could be open to interpretation as creative and directional under the symbol of the Kingdom of God with the emergence at a later stage of evolution of actual self-awareness with historical man.[56] To my mind, in order to be consistent, the symbol of the Kingdom needs to be extended to cover this possibility, and this Teilhard's theory, understood as myth, allows. In this it is thoroughly cosmic, and reflects the perspective of the Pauline myth Teilhard used as his own source of inspiration:

> For the creation waits with eager longing for the reveal-
> ing of the sons of God; . . . because the creation itself
> will be set free from its bondage to decay and obtain the
> glorious liberty of the children of God. We know that
> the whole creation has been groaning in travail together
> until now. . . .[57]

Tillich's reason for favoring "potential self-awareness" rather than actual self-awareness with respect to the inanimate, as his statement previously quoted indicates, is because the latter cannot be verified. However, "potential self-awareness" is subject to the same limitation. If he wishes to take verification seriously, and there is no reason why he should, his position is no way improved by being merely potential.

For both Teilhard and Tillich the level of dimension of consciousness is of vital importance. With increased conscious-ness[58] there is increased centeredness, and this has cosmic signifi-cance. Tillich strikes a very Teilhardian note when he says:

> The centered self is dependent not only on the influences
> of its social surroundings which are constantly given and
> received but also on those which are effective in society
> without being apprehended and formulated. All this shows
> that the independence within an individual is only half the
> truth.
>
> Biological, psychological, and sociological powers are
> effective in every individual decision. The universe works
> through us as part of the universe.[59]

This notion reflects Teilhard's theme that through the con-sciousness of man the universe knows itself, though he elaborates this further in his doctrine of the noosphere.

For Tillich, "history-bearing groups are characterized by their ability to act in a centered way,"[60] leading to his view of communities. The more centered the community, the more organized it is, and the more its component members are bound together by "eros"[61] which underlies the organizational form.

> Blood relations, language, traditions, and memories create many forms of "eros" which make the power structure possible. Preservation by enforcement and increase by conquest follow, but do not produce, the historical power of the group. The element of compulsion in every historical power structure is not its foundation but an unavoidable condition of its existence. It is at the same time the cause of its destruction if the "eros" relations disappear or are completely replaced by force.[62]

This is very similar to Teilhard's theory of growing organization and socialization prompted and held together by "love". Teilhard, of course, continues his analysis in terms of the logic of evolution so that this process plays a critical part in the achievement of the Omega point. Tillich makes no necessary connection between this process and the coming of the Kingdom of God and its actualization with the end of History. However, he does not explicitly rule out a growth in unity as history goes forward. His main concern is to say that there can be no unity within history, and in posthistory neither unity nor disunity is a question.[63]

I do not think there is any fundamental difference between the respective positions, though Teilhard's is far more detailed as it represents a central theme in his thesis, and of far wider application, for his "history-bearing" groups cover the whole period of evolution.

OMEGA AND LOGOS: THE GROUND OF THE MYTH

I have endeavored to open up Teilhard's evolutionary phenomenology to the metaphysical insights of Tillich's myth of history under the symbol of the Kingdom of God, to show that

difficulties surrounding the "signification" that Teilhard finds in the "ontic" world from the perspective of biology largely disappear when we change our perspective to that of the Kingdom of God, that is, to the eschatological viewpoint. This must always be recognized for what it is: the answer given by reasonable faith to the ambiguities of the empirical world; a faith that, while not disagreeing with descriptive facts, dares to transcend those facts to seek their ultimate purpose and meaning. However, for this procedure to be other than the desperate seeking of the already lost, there must be concrete justification for the faith involved. The final step in my attempted synthesis of Teilhard's and Tillich's theories is concerned with just this point.

"Omega" and "Logos" are the respective symbols under which Teilhard and Tillich approach the universal or cosmic implications of the Kingdom of God active in human history. This activity is actualized and made explicit in a single historical event, the Incarnation. For both of them this provides a locus, a center, for the universe. This is the manifestation of the Kingdom of God that justifies our myth. It is this that makes possible a Christian theology, and not just *a* theology, but as Tillich says, *the* theology. He says,

> The basis of this claim is the Christian doctrine that the Logos became flesh, that the principle of the divine self-revelation became manifest in the event "Jesus as the Christ". If this message is true, Christian theology has received a foundation that transcends the foundation of any other theology and which itself cannot be transcended. Christian theology has received something that is absolutely concrete and absolutely universal at the same time. No myth, no mystical vision, no metaphysical principle, no sacred law, has the concreteness of a personal life. In comparison with a personal life everything else is relatively abstract. And none of these relatively abstract foundations of theology has the universality of the Logos, which itself is the principle of universality. In comparison with

95

the Logos everything else is relatively particular. Christian theology is *the* theology in so far as it is based on the tension between the absolutely concrete and the absolutely universal. . . . Only that which has the power of representing everything particular is absolutely concrete. And only that which has the power of representing everything abstract is absolutely universal. This leads to a point where the absolutely concrete and the absolutely universal are identical. And this is the point at which Christian theology emerges, the point which is described as the "Logos who has become flesh."[64]

The "Logos" or "Omega" event within history is that which makes history possible. It is the only descriptive, empirical fact of the "ontic world" that of itself is eternally significant. It transcends itself. It becomes its own symbol, and a symbol under which all other empirical phenomena can find significance. As such it is the center of the universe, the center of history. But as Tillich says:

The appearance of Jesus as the Christ is the historical event in which history becomes aware of itself and its meaning. There is — even for an empirical and relativistic approach — no other event of which this *could* be asserted. But the *actual* assertion remains a matter of daring faith.[65]

Teilhard echoes this in many places, for example:

Omega . . . coincides concretely with the point called the Parousia of Christ. . . . It is the supreme event, when, as faith tells us, history is to be welded to the Transcendent, that the mystery of the Incarnation culminates and asserts itself in the realism of a physical interpretation of the universe.[66]

The identification of Christ with Omega, with Logos, in the Incarnation, under the symbol of the Kingdom of God is centered in the one transcending, concrete event, the Incarnation. Our myth is anchored in this reality. Our symbol is operative only in terms of it. The key to the myth must always be a response in faith to the confrontation of Jesus of Nazareth with the world in the central question of life, "What think ye of Christ?"

CONCLUSION

W. A. Whitehouse indicated,[67] with respect to the uneasy truce that exists between science and theology, that "the felt need, as expressed by many acute and sensitive persons, is not for a synthesis, but for a theology standing on its own right but expressed with greater openness toward the physical sciences."[68] He describes Teilhard de Chardin's proposed synthesis as being of "disputed worth," and in this he is undoubtedly correct.

However, when we put aside Teilhard's theory as an empirical synthesis, and see in it elements of a modern creation myth, opening up history and "being-as-becoming" under the symbol of the Kingdom of God, I do think that we have theological ground on which to stand, and which does have a greater openness to the physical sciences by seeing them under their own related "myth of objectification." Thus the tentative character of all knowledge is recognized; but it is tentative not because it may be untrue, but because it is dynamic and open to a future led on by hope, that is justified by a mythology that accounts not only for man's experience of the world but also his own felt experience of transcendence. Through myth each of these experiences can be seen to be equally valid and meaningful.

There is no longer a world in which man is faced with the traumatic experience of a reality somehow superior to his own, to which he does not really belong. The felt unity of man with the world is no longer denied by a dualism which will in no way allow it; for dualism is itself the product of myth, and on another level, the level of signification, it can be transcended by myth, the myth of "being-as-becoming."

LET US LEAVE THE SURFACE AND,
WITHOUT LEAVING THE WORLD,
PLUNGE INTO GOD.

Tillich recognized that a "theology of the inorganic is lacking," and that the "religious significance of the inorganic is immense, but rarely considered by theology."[69] His own attempt to do so was limited by an intellectual orientation which was not that of the physical sciences, and so he does not have the basic information to develop a thoroughgoing theology of the inorganic, though he does so tentatively while recognizing the need for further expansion. He sees quite clearly that the theory of evolution plays an important role in exposing the possibility of a viable alternative to modern materialism with its ontology of death, which consequently failed to take sufficient heed to the "within of things," namely, life itself. For Tillich this was an alternative in which the ambiguities of life can be transcended.

In this he is in remarkable agreement with Jonas. In a sense, Jonas provides the link between Tillich and Teilhard, allowing Teilhard's phenomenology a surer metaphysical foundation in myth, and so permitting aspects of Teilhard's and Tillich's theology to come together on more certain ground.

Tillich's position is thus modified by Teilhard's more thoroughgoing view of evolution, and Teilhard's theology by Tillich's philosophical basis for theology. The possibility is now open for a theology of the inorganic which does not see it in fundamental discontinuity with the organic. We are thus able to think in terms of a comprehensive theology of nature, a theology that recognizes the sort of "factuality" that both science and faith refer to, and the connection between them. Such a theology, as Langmead Casserley has said, "we can now see to be indispensable, not only for apologetic purposes, but also for the intellectual completeness of our theology itself."[70]

NOTES FOR "TEILHARD DE CHARDIN AS PHILOSOPHER OF HISTORY," BY ROBERT V. WILSHIRE

1. Mooney, Christopher, *Teilhard de Chardin and the Mystery of Christ,* (New York, Harper & Row, 1966), p. 25.
2. Jonas, Hans, *The Phenomenon of Life,* (New York, Harper & Row, 1951), p. 7.
3. *Ibid.,* p. 8.
4. *Ibid.,* pp. 26-33, pp. 135-152.
5. *Ibid.,* pp. 17-18.
6. *Ibid.,* p. 55.
7. *Ibid.,* p. 57.
8. *Ibid.,* pp. 38-58.
9. *Ibid.,* pp. 43-49.
10. *Ibid.,* p. 49.
11. *Ibid.,* p. 213, from Blaise Pascal, *Pensees.*
12. Pascal, Blaise, *Pensees,* tr., W.F. Trotter, (New York, Washington Square Press, 1941), p. 116.
13. I Corinthians, 15:47.
14. Jonas, Hans, *The Phenomenon of Life,* pp. 87-91.
15. *Ibid.,* pp. 208-209.
16. *Ibid.,* p. 6.
17. *Ibid.,* p. 58.
18. *Ibid.,* p. 261.
19. *Ibid.,* p. x.
20. *Ibid.,* pp. 271-281.
21. Farrer, Austin, *Thoeria to Thoery,* Vol. 1, October, 1966.
22. MacIntyre, Alasdair C., *Difficulties of Christian Belief,* (London, Student Christian Movement Press, 1959), pp. 74-97.
23. I Corinthians, 13:12.
24. Schoonenberg, Peter, *God's World in the Making.* (Pittsburgh, Pa., Divine Word Publications, 1964), pp. 5-6.
25. Zaehner, R.C., ed., *Hindu Scriptures,* Everyman's Library, 944, (New York, Dutton, 1966), X, xc; X, cxxi; and X, cxxix.
26. I realize that there is not much scholarly opinion which supports the view that the origins of the Genesis creation myths in their Hebrew form pre-dates the Babylonian exile. However, my statement could be adjusted to take account of this. It should also be noted that the word 'science' is being used here in a very broad sense.
27. Tillich, Paul, *Systematic Theology,* I, (Chicago, Harper & Row, 1951), pp. 78-81.
28. Ayre, A.J., *Language, Truth, and Logic,* 2nd ed., (London, Gollancz, 1946), Chapters 1 and 6.
29. Tillich, Paul, *Systematic Theology,* I, p. 16.
30. Tillich, Paul, *Systematic Theology,* III.
31. *Ibid.,* III, p. 300
32. *Ibid.,* III, pp. 332-333.
33. *Ibid.,* I, pp. 275-276.
34. *Ibid.,* I, pp. 275-276.
35. *Ibid.,* I, p. 209.
36. *Ibid.,* III, pp. 107-109.

37. *Ibid.*, III, p. 357.
38. *Ibid.*, III, p. 307-309.
39. *Ibid.*, III, p. 394.
40. *Ibid.*, I, pp. 30-31.
41. *Ibid.*, III, p. 359.
42. *Ibid.*, III, pp. 333-339.
43. *Ibid.*, III, pp. 12-17
44. *Ibid.*, III, p. 357.
45. *Ibid.*, II, p. 96.
46. *Ibid.*, II, p. 97.
47. Mascall, Eric, *Christian Theology and Natural Science*, (London, Longman, Green, & Co., 1956).
48. Mooney, Christopher, pp. 97-100.
49. *Ibid.*, pp. 34-35.
50. Teilhard de Chardin, Pierre, *Oeuvres*, "Mon Univers," (Paris, Seuil, 1955-65), ix, pp. 65-114.
51. Tillich, Paul, *Systematic Theology*, III, pp. 20-21.
52. *Ibid.*, III, p. 305.
53. It would seem, therefore, pertinent to ask what is the difference between the actuality of the potential that will never be fulfilled and the actuality that will be fulfilled. I don't really think the question can be answered. It would seem to be stretching the definition of "actual" to apply it in any way to that which will never be.
54. Tillich, Paul, *Systematic Theology*, II, pp. 120-121.
55. *Ibid.*, III, p. 336.
56. *Ibid.*, III, p. 84.
57. *Romans*, 8:19-22.
58. Tillich, Paul, *Systematic Theology*, III, pp. 26-27.
59. *Ibid.*, II, p. 42.
60. *Ibid.*, III, p. 308.
61. It would seem that Tillich means by "eros" much the same thing as Teilhard when the latter uses the much more general "love."
62. *Ibid.*, III, p. 309.
63. *Ibid.*, III, pp. 311-312.
64. *Ibid.*, I, p. 16.
65. *Ibid.*, III, pp. 368-369.
66. Mooney, Christopher, p. 182, from Teilhard de Chardin, *Trois Choses Que Je Vois*.
67. Jenkins, Daniel T., ed., *The Scope of Theology*, (New York, World Publishers, 1968).
68. *Ibid.*, p. 155.
69. Tillich, Paul, *Systematic Theology*, III, pp. 18-19.
70. Casserly, Langmead, *Graceful Reason*, (Greenwich, Conn., Longmans, 1954), p. 145.

WE CAN NO LONGER MEASURE OUR
EFFORTS BY OLD ACHIEVEMENTS, NO
MATTER HOW EXALTING THESE
   WERE IN THEIR OWN TIME.